Why Marriage?

Anne –
You'll always
be my hero!
Thanks for
fighting and
winning for
all of us.
Matt

Anna —
you'll always
be my boy!

Reflecting over
Winning the
old pro.

Mom

Why Marriage?

The history
shaping today's debate
over gay equality

To Ame,
with great admiration for
the magnificent work you're
doing!

George Chauncey

George Chauncey

BASIC
BOOKS

A Member of the Perseus Books Group

New York

Hardcover first published in 2004 by Basic Books,
A Member of the Perseus Books Group
Paperback first published in 2005 by Basic Books

Books published by Basic Books are available at special discounts for
bulk purchases in the United States by corporations, institutions, and
other organizations. For more information, please contact the
Special Markets Department at the Perseus Books Group, 11 Cambridge Center,
Cambridge, MA 02142, or call (617) 252-5298, (800) 255-1514,
or e-mail special.markets@perseusbooks.com.

Library of Congress Cataloging-in-Publication Data
Chauncey, George.
Why marriage? : the history shaping today's debate over gay equality /
George Chauncey.
p. cm.
Includes bibliographical references and index.
HC: ISBN-13 978-0-465-00957-2; ISBN 0-465-00957-3 (alk. paper)
1. Gay rights—United States. 2. Same-sex marriage—United States.
3. Same-sex marriage—Law and legislation—United States.
4. Homophobia—United States. I. Title.
HQ76.8.U5C43   2004
306.76'6'0973—DC22
2004014747

Design by Jane Raese
Set in 11.5-point Janson

PBK: ISBN-13 978-0-465-00958-9; ISBN 0-465-00958-1
05 06 07 08 / 10 9 8 7 6 5 4 3 2 1

To Mary Bonauto and Jenny Wriggins

Contents

Preface

M ORE THAN TWO YEARS after lesbian and gay couples won the right to marry in Massachusetts—the momentous event that both inspired this book and concludes the history it tells—gay marriage remains a contentious issue in American life and politics. The Massachusetts decision produced a thunderous reaction from leaders of the Christian Right, who made sure the issue reverberated through the 2004 presidential campaign and in battles over state marriage referenda, which they initiated across the nation. By the end of 2004, it often seemed that antigay activists had seized the upper hand. But from a long-term historical perspective, the present situation appears more complex.

There is no escaping the fact that the advocates of marriage equality for lesbian and gay couples were trounced in the November 2004 election. Voters in eleven states amended their constitutions to prohibit gay marriage. No one expected a different outcome in inhospitable states such as Mississippi, Oklahoma, Arkansas, North Dakota, and Utah. Ten of the eleven states already had antigay marriage laws on the books. But even in Oregon, the one state where a major campaign was organized against the amendment and where activists thought it might be defeated, the amendment passed by a smaller, though still decisive, margin of 57–43 percent. Seeing a chance to turn the tide against the growing public acceptance of gay people, the Christian Right quickly mobilized to put constitutional amendments on the ballot in other states.

Although the amendments' sponsors zeroed in on (and elevated) many voters' discomfort with the idea of gay marriage, the expansive wording of the amendments exposed their broader right-wing agenda. The majority of the amendments threatened to roll back a host of policies put in place in recent years to address the needs of gay couples and unmarried heterosexual couples as well. Eleven of the seventeen states that amended their constitutions before 2005 did so with language that sweepingly prohibits *any* "legal status identical or substantially similar to that of marriage" (Kentucky) or "a legal status for relationships of unmarried individuals that intends to approximate the design, qualities, significance or effect of marriage" (Ohio). The broad wording of such amendments immediately jeapordized legal arrangements, including domestic partnership programs, offered by private and public employers, to unmarried heterosexual as well as gay couples, if they "approximate the . . . design . . . or effect of marriage." Only litigation will tell just how many rights these amendments will take away or preclude. But shortly after Michigan voters passed such an amendment, Governor Jennifer Granholm suspended a new labor contract provision providing domestic partnership benefits to state government employees. In Ohio, a judge threw out a domestic violence felony charge against a man who had been accused of assaulting his girlfriend, explaining that the Ohio constitutional amendment prohibited the extension of domestic violence protections to unmarried couples (other judges disagreed, and the ultimate outcome remains uncertain). In Missouri and Utah, campaigns to enact domestic partnership programs were cut short.[1] By playing on voters' unfamiliarity with the reality of gay couples' lives and repeatedly warning that the extension of marital rights to them would somehow undermine heterosexual voters' marriages, the amendments' proponents struck a major blow against policies that deal humanely with the diverse realities of families.

The decisive margins by which the amendments succeeded make it clear that the advocates of gay marriage have a rough road ahead of them. This shouldn't be surprising. Any civil rights movement that advocates major change in existing social arrangements elicits a powerful reaction. Just fifty years ago, the Supreme Court's decision in *Brown v. Board of Education*, which ruled that states could no longer establish racially segregated school systems, produced an even more thunderous reaction that included massive resistance by southern state governments, an upsurge in racist organizing by the Ku Klux Klan and White Citizens Councils, and heated attacks on the courts, which were portrayed as antidemocratic institutions that had usurped the popular will.

Civil rights movements are never "well timed" because any significant movement causes discomfort and dismay and gets in the way of normal politics. That's why when we look at the history of those movements, we honor the people who had the moral imagination to envision a different and more just world, and the moral courage to fight for it, even though their contemporaries thought they were dangerous upstarts, ill-advised, and impolitic at best.

Nonetheless, as a historian I am most struck by how quickly public opinion is changing in regard to the recognition of same-sex relationships. The campaign for marriage equality has not just produced a backlash. It has pushed the national conversation about gay life and equality much further forward than seemed possible just five years ago.

The dramatic shift in public attitudes was even reflected in the 2004 Bush campaign. Admittedly, this is not how that campaign is usually remembered. On the morning after President Bush won reelection, most reporters were startled to learn that exit polls showed 22 percent of voters cited "moral values" as their chief concern. Many of them took this as proof of the Christian Right's claim that a massive outpouring of new evangelical voters—outraged at the prospect of gay marriage—had turned the tide against Democratic contender John Kerry. It wasn't surprising to hear Christian Right leaders portray themselves as the leaders of a vast and newly mobilized constituency, since this claim bolstered the political clout they needed both to push their legislative agenda through Congress and to help ensure the appointment of conservative Supreme Court justices who would reverse *Roe v. Wade.* Their claim also generated a defeatist attitude among gay activists and divided their allies, many of whom blamed lesbians and gay men for asking for too much, too quickly. But it was more surprising to see how many reporters initially accepted the Christian Right's self-serving political spin on the election outcome and, by repeating it, gave it the status of political "fact."

In the weeks following the election, more dispassionate analysis of the vote by political scientists discredited the Christian Right's claims. For starters, the president's margin increased 2.9 percent over his 2000 margin in the 39 states *without* marriage initiatives on the ballot, but only 2.6 percent in the 11 states *with* marriage on the ballot. Even in Ohio, the hotly contested state where it initially appeared that the gay marriage referendum had tipped the election to Bush by inspiring an unprecedented outpouring of white evangelical voters, further analysis showed that the share of voters who attended church once or more a week (the best measure of voters who might be religiously inspired) declined to 40 percent in 2004, compared to 45 percent in 2000.[2] Although most morning-after-the-election commentators accepted the Christian Right's claim that concern for "moral values" signified opposition to abortion and gay marriage, one poll showed that 42 percent of "morals" voters said the war in Iraq was the most important moral issue influencing their vote, compared to 13 percent who chose abortion and less than 10 percent who cited gay marriage.[3] This shouldn't have been surprising. One reason President Bush won such fervent support from many white evangelicals was that he framed most issues in moral terms, and he often justified the war by claiming that America was acting as God's agent to spread freedom in Iraq and throughout the world.

Even more strikingly, whatever moral values meant to voters in 2004, they were less significant a factor than in other recent elections, before marriage became a major issue and before the September 11 attacks transformed the political landscape. In 1996, fully half of presidential voters chose either abortion or "family values" as their top issues.[4] But in 2004, security issues—Iraq and terrorism together—were cited by more voters (34 percent) than were moral issues. Whatever voters meant by moral issues, there is no reliable indication that the marriage issue played a decisive role in the election.

After all the post-election spin, it is hard to remember that the Bush campaign downplayed its appeal to the Christian Right during the election itself. Under intense pressure from Christian Right leaders, the president announced his support for a constitutional amendment, but he barely mentioned it during the campaign because his advisors realized that the issue cut both ways, and his appearing too hostile or intolerant of gay people would cost him votes.

Look at the 2004 Republican convention, which shaped the election's dynamics so decisively in the president's favor that not even his weak performance in the debates could derail him. The convention's organizers framed the election as a referendum on John Kerry's capacity to protect the country from terrorism, not as a referendum on marriage. One prominent speaker after another sought to persuade undecided voters that no matter how much they might disagree with the president on other issues (which were rarely specified but presumably included "moral issues" such as gay marriage, abortion, and the separation of church and state), they should rally around him as a resolute and forthright leader. Indeed, the convention's organizers filled prime-time television with Republican moderates like former New York Mayor Rudolph Giuliani, Senator John McCain, and Governors Arnold Schwarzenegger and George Pataki, all of whom were known to oppose the constitutional amendment endorsed by the convention platform. Georgia Democratic Senator Zell Miller and the presidential nominee himself were the only prime-time speakers who supported the constitutional amendment, and even the president's acceptance speech—like his stump speech on the campaign trail—devoted only one sentence to the issue. The sentence produced thunderous applause from the evangelicals who were primed to hear it, but barely registered with most other voters. The fear of terrorism spawned by September 11 and Republican charges that John Kerry was a "flip-flopper" who couldn't be trusted to act resolutely in a time of war dominated the convention and won the president's reelection. Kerry's refusal to take a decisive stand on the difficult issue of marriage only made him more vulnerable to the charge that he was an indecisive flip-flopper without a strong internal compass.

Other steps show how carefully the Republican ticket handled gay issues during the campaign. Two months before Senator Kerry was pilloried for mentioning Mary Cheney's lesbianism, Vice President Dick Cheney gave an emotionally compelling account of his lesbian daughter to help explain his personal opposition to a constitutional amendment on marriage and to give the Republican ticket an aura of tolerance and inclusivity that its political platform belied. In the closing days of the campaign, even President Bush sought to moderate his image by supporting the right of states to enact civil unions for gay couples, something his own platform and eight of the eleven state constitutional amendments passed on election day would prohibit.

Why? Because Bush's advisors believed that as important as it was to mobilize evangelical voters and as safe as it was to do so by emphasizing the president's own evangelical faith and use of moral language, displaying too much obeisance to the Christian Right's cultural program risked trouble.

They had reason to believe this. For three decades now, as this book shows, evangelical voters committed to "traditional family values" have played an important, but polarizing, electoral role. They were credited with helping to elect Ronald Reagan in 1980 and playing a significant role in the Republican takeover of Congress in 1994. But the organizers of this year's Republican convention kept the Christian Right out of the spotlight because they were determined to avoid the disastrous mistake of the 1992 convention, which sabotaged George W.H. Bush's reelection by giving center stage to cultural conservatives promising a "culture war" for the "soul of America." They knew full well that in the twelve years since Patrick Buchanan's harsh antigay rhetoric had frightened voters away from the Republican Party, the public's acceptance of gay people had only grown.

Indeed, while support for gay marriage remains a distinctly minority position, the more remarkable fact is that such support is growing steadily as people become more familiar with the idea and more informed about what is at stake for gay couples and their children. The seachange in public opinion has been reflected in the positions of politicians and the actions of state governments. As recently as 2000, civil unions seemed a radical idea, and Vermont's Governor Howard Dean was denounced for supporting them. But people noticed that the sky did not fall in Vermont when civil unions were established, and within a few years support for them had become a mainstream position. Every major Democratic candidate for president supported civil unions in the 2004 primaries, something that would have been unthinkable just four years earlier.

Although many observers declared that the state constitutional amendments had stopped the pro-marriage movement in its tracks, promising court cases continued to advance in California, Connecticut, New Jersey, and several other states. More telling evidence of the growing public support for gay couples was provided by several state legislatures. The legislatures of New Jersey and Maine passed laws providing a degree of recognition and security to gay couples. Then California's legislature enacted a sweeping domestic partnership law that granted registered gay couples all of the state benefits available to married couples (though, of course, none of the many federal benefits), and two years later came within a few votes of enacting marriage itself for gay couples. Connecticut's legislature, with support from the Republican governor, enacted a similarly sweeping civil union law. Early in 2005, the national governing body of the United Church of Christ decisively embraced marriage for gay couples as a religious as well as a civil matter. At about the same time, Canada and Spain joined Sweden and Denmark in granting full marriage equality to gay couples—another indication that the United States was increasingly out of step with the "western civilization" conservatives so often invoked in cultural debate.

Whether or not lesbians and gay men should be allowed to adopt children or teach them were the two most explosive gay rights issues before marriage entered the scene, as this book shows. There has been a dramatic growth in public support for gay people's right to do both, but only after a generation of debate and education eroded old stereotypes and fears. Gay marriage is a much newer issue to most people and still evokes as much uncertainty and anxiety as the idea of gay teachers and parents, or even gay characters on television sitcoms, did just a generation ago. But as people have become more familiar with the lives of their gay relatives and neighbors and more aware of the immense range of rights, protections, benefits, and obligations conferred to couples by marriage and marriage alone, they have also become more supportive of gay people's quest for legal security for their relationships. Even as voters passed antigay marriage amendments in eleven mostly conservative states on election day 2004, exit polls showed that 60 percent of voters nationwide supported either civil unions (35 percent) or marriage (25 percent) for gay couples, a 50 percent increase in support since the 2000 election. The generational shift is especially noteworthy: Americans in their late teens and twenties are four times more likely to support gay marriage than their grandparents are.

The Christian Right claims that amending the constitution serves to preserve democratic rule against the proclivities of activist judges. But, in fact, their amendments subvert the democratic process by foreclosing the national debate over marriage, which has only just begun and has already resulted in a decisive growth in support for the rights of gay couples. The opponents of the dozen amendments passed in 2004 had far too little time to present their case to voters. Amending the constitution to prohibit gay marriage would impose the more hostile attitudes of the past on the generations of the future by writing them into the fundamental law of the land.

This is precisely the goal of the Christian Right, and consequently, these are especially perilous times despite the steady growth of support for gay people and their families. Although a federal constitutional amendment seems unlikely to pass, it is all too likely that many more state amendments will pass in the next few years. Unless the gay movement and its supporters respond more effectively to this challenge, they will face a monumental new roadblock that will slow progress for a generation to come.

Still, as the passionate opposition to abortion reminds us, there's nothing like seeing your most precious moral values threatened to galvanize a movement. As the marriage debate continues, people will realize how many of the state constitutional amendments ban not only marriage but all of the rights and protections associated with marriage. Soon enough, they'll hear about a friend who cannot make medical decisions for his incapacitated partner or be with him in the hospital trauma center because the law requires them to be treated as legal strangers. Or, they'll learn that the colleague down the hall at work can't use the company's medical plan to provide health insurance to the children she is raising with her partner. Or, they'll hear about an elderly woman at church who lost her home and financial security when her partner died because the IRS wouldn't grant her a marital exemption from estate taxes, and she had no right to her partner's social security benefits.

Growing numbers of people are deeply offended, even outraged, by such injustices. Republicans risk squandering their chance of building an enduring majority if, in their eagerness to reward a core constituency—the Christian Right, they forget how quickly the public's support for full gay equality is growing. And Democrats who run away from their commitment to civil rights will demoralize one of their own core constituencies: not just millions of gay voters, but millions of heterosexuals who cherish their gay nephews, sisters, friends, and teachers, and for whom justice, compassion, fairness, and equality are fundamental moral values.

Introduction:
Why Marriage?

THE YEAR STRETCHING from the spring of 2003 to the
spring of 2004 was a decisive turning point in the history of lesbians and gay men in the United States. In June
2003 the Supreme Court issued a landmark ruling in the case
of *Lawrence v. Texas* that overturned the nation's remaining
sodomy laws and extended the right to privacy—which includes the right to make decisions about one's intimate life—
to lesbians and gay men. The decision was hailed—and denounced—as a sign of the dramatic shift in attitudes toward
lesbians and gays. Just seventeen years earlier in its *Bowers v.
Hardwick* ruling, the Court had dismissed the claim that anyone had a right to engage in homosexual activity as "facetious." In *Lawrence*, Justice Anthony Kennedy embraced
the "liberty" of gay people to form relationships, "whether or
not [they are] entitled to formal recognition in the law," and
condemned the *Bowers* decision for "demean[ing] the lives of
homosexual persons."

The *Lawrence* decision produced a thunderous outcry from
the nation's right-wing congressmen and religious leaders.

Above all, they feared that the decision's expansive language made marriage rights for gay couples the logical next step, as Justice Antonin Scalia warned in his scathing dissent. But Republican Congressional leaders were not just reacting to *Lawrence* when they hastily announced their plans to push for a constitutional amendment codifying marriage as a relationship between a man and a woman. Everywhere that spring there were signs that conservatives were losing the long-running debate over the place of gay people in society. Two Canadian provinces legally recognized same-sex marriages shortly before *Lawrence* was announced; the Episcopal Church risked schism by deciding to ordain an openly gay bishop; and even Wal-Mart added sexual orientation to its written antidiscrimination policy.

That November, the Supreme Judicial Court of Massachusetts cited *Lawrence* when it ruled that same-sex couples should have the same access to the benefits of marriage that mixed-sex couples enjoy. The contentious debate that erupted in Massachusetts over various state constitutional amendments that would deny this equality to gay couples, the decision of local elected officials in San Francisco, Portland, New Paltz, and other municipalities to marry or issue marriage licenses to such couples, the extraordinary spectacle of thousands of same-sex couples lining up to take advantage of that promise, and the equally stunning spectacle of the president of the United States calling for a constitutional amendment that would inscribe inequality into the fundamental law of the land—all ensure that the issues that dominated the summer of 2003 will continue to occupy us well past the summer of 2004.

The debate is now fully engaged and has made this a decisive moment for our generation.

To casual observers, these momentous events may appear to have come out of nowhere. But in fact they have a history, and our understanding of them is impoverished so long as we ignore that history. Today's marriage debate is shaped by half a century of struggle over the place of lesbians and gay men in American society and an even longer history of evolution in the meaning and legal character of marriage itself. The gay quest for equal rights in marriage, always a contentious issue within the gay movement itself, gained impetus because of the profound changes wrought in lesbian and gay life in the 1980s and 1990s by the AIDS crisis and the boom in lesbian and gay parenting. The response to that quest was shaped by the palpable shift in heterosexual attitudes toward lesbians and gay men during the same years and by the complex and interrelated histories of civil rights, gay rights, and women's rights. No historical study can resolve the debate over marriage, but this one aims to illuminate how we came to this moment and what is at stake in this debate.

ONE

The Legacy of Antigay Discrimination

*T*HE PLACE OF LESBIANS AND GAY MEN in American society has dramatically changed in the last half century.
The change has been so profound that the harsh discrimination once faced by gay people has virtually disappeared from
popular memory. That history bears repeating, since its
legacy shapes today's debate over marriage.

Although most people recognize that gay life was difficult
before the growth of the gay movement in the 1970s, they often have only the vaguest sense of why: that gay people were
scorned and ridiculed, made to feel ashamed, afraid, and
alone. But antigay discrimination was much more systematic
and powerful than this.

Fifty years ago, there was no *Will & Grace* or *Ellen*, no *Queer
Eye for the Straight Guy*, no *Philadelphia* or *The Hours*, no annual Lesbian, Gay, Bisexual, and Transgender (LGBT) film
festival. In fact, Hollywood films were *prohibited* from including lesbian or gay characters, discussing gay themes, or even
inferring the existence of homosexuality. The Hollywood stu-
dios established these rules (popularly known as the Hays

Code) in the 1930s under pressure from a censorship movement led by Catholic and other religious leaders, who threatened them with mass boycotts and restrictive federal legislation. The absolute ban on gay representation, vigorously
enforced by Hollywood's own censorship board, remained in
effect for some thirty years and effectively prohibited the discussion of homosexuality in the most important medium of
the mid-twentieth century, even though some filmmakers
found subtle ways to subvert it.[1]

Censorship extended to the stage as well. In 1927, after a
serious lesbian drama opened on Broadway to critical acclaim—and after Mae West announced that she planned to
open a play called *The Drag*—New York state passed a "pad-
lock law" that threatened to shut down for a year any theater
that dared to stage a play with lesbian or gay characters.
Given Broadway's national importance as a staging ground
for new plays, this law had dramatic effects on American theater for a generation.[2]

Fifty years ago, no openly gay people worked for the federal government. In fact, shortly after he became president in
1953, Dwight Eisenhower issued an executive order that
banned homosexuals from government employment, civilian
as well as military, and required companies with government
contracts to ferret out and fire their gay employees. At the
height of the McCarthy witch-hunt, the U.S. State Department fired more homosexuals than communists. In the 1950s
and 1960s literally thousands of men and women were discharged or forced to resign from civilian positions in the federal government because they were suspected of being gay or
lesbian.[3] It was only in 1975 that the ban on gay federal em-

ployees was lifted, and it took until the late 1990s before such discrimination in federal hiring was prohibited.

Fifty years ago, countless teachers, hospital workers, and other state and municipal employees also lost their jobs as a result of official policy. Beginning in 1958, for instance, the Florida Legislative Investigation Committee, which had been established by the legislature in 1956 to investigate and discredit civil rights activists, turned its attention to homosexuals working in the state's universities and public schools. Its initial investigation of the University of Florida resulted in the dismissal of fourteen faculty and staff members, and in the next five years it interrogated some 320 suspected gay men and lesbians. Under pressure from the committee, numerous teachers gave up their jobs and countless students were forced to drop out of college.[4]

Fifty years ago, there were no gay business associations or gay bars advertising in newspapers. In fact, many gay-oriented businesses were illegal and gay people had no right to public assembly. In many states, following the repeal of prohibition in 1933, it even became illegal for restaurants and bars to serve lesbians or gay men. The New York State Liquor Authority, for instance, issued regulations prohibiting bars, restaurants, cabarets, and other establishments with liquor licenses from employing or serving homosexuals or allowing homosexuals to congregate on their premises.[5] The Authority's rationale was that the mere presence of homosexuals made an establishment "disorderly," and when the courts rejected that argument the Authority began using evidence gathered by plainclothes investigators of one man trying to pick up another or of patrons' unconventional gender behavior to provide proof of a bar's disorderly character.[6] One bar in Times Square was closed in 1939, for instance, because the Liquor Authority alleged it "permitted the premises to become disorderly in permitting homosexuals, degenerates and other undesirable people to congregate on the premises." A Brooklyn bar was closed in 1960 because it became "a gathering place for homosexuals and degenerates who conducted themselves in an offensive and indecent manner" by, among other things, "wearing tight fitting trousers," walking "with a sway to their hips," and "gesturing with limp wrists." A bar in upstate New York was closed in 1963 after an investigator observed "two females, one mannish in appearance, [who was] holding the hands of the other female."[7]

Any restaurant or bar that gained a gay reputation faced constant harassment and police raids until the police shut it down for good. Some bars in New York and Los Angeles posted signs telling potential gay customers: *If You Are Gay, Please Stay Away*, or, more directly, *We Do Not Serve Homosexuals*. In the thirty-odd years between the enactment of such regulations by New York state in 1933 and their rejection by the New York state courts in the mid-1960s, the police closed *hundreds* of bars that had tolerated gay customers in New York City alone.[8]

Fifty years ago, elected officials did not court the gay vote and the nation's mayors did not proclaim LGBT Pride Week. Instead, many mayors periodically declared war on homosexuals—or sex deviates, as they were usually called. In many cities, gay residents knew that if the mayor needed to show he was tough on crime and vice just before an election, he would order a crackdown on gay bars. Hundreds of people would be arrested. Their names put in the paper. Their meeting places closed. This did not just happen once or twice, or just in smaller cities. Rather, it happened regularly in every major city, from New York and Miami to Chicago, San Francisco, and LA. After his administration's commitment to suppressing gay life became an issue in his 1959 re-election campaign, San Francisco's mayor launched a two-year-long crackdown on the city's gay bars and other meeting places. Forty to sixty men and women were arrested every week in bar sweeps, and within two years almost a third of the city's gay bars had been closed.[9] Miami's gay scene was relentlessly attacked by the police and press in 1954. New York launched major crackdowns on gay bars as part of its campaign to "clean up the city" before both the 1939 and 1964 World's Fairs. During the course of a 1955 investigation of the gay scene in Boise, Idaho, 1,400 people were interrogated and coerced into identifying the names of other gay residents.[10] Across America, homosexuals were an easy target, with few allies.

Fifty years ago, there was no mass LGBT movement. In fact, the handful of early gay activists risked everything to speak up for their rights. When the police learned of the country's earliest known gay political group, which had been established by a postal worker in Chicago in 1924, they raided his home and seized his group's files and membership list. A quarter century later, when the first national gay rights group, the Mattachine Society, was founded, it repeatedly had to reassure its anxious members that the police would not seize its membership list. The U.S. Post Office banned its newspaper from the mails in 1954, and in some cities the police shut down newstands that dared to carry it. In 1959, a few weeks after Mattachine held its first press conference during a national convention in Denver, the police raided the homes of three of its Denver organizers; one lost his job and spent sixty days in jail. Such harassment and censorship of free speech made it difficult for people to organize or speak on their own behalf and for all Americans to debate and learn about gay issues.[11]

Fifty years ago, no state had a gay rights law. Rather, every state had a sodomy law and other laws penalizing homosexual conduct. Beginning in the late nineteenth century, municipal police forces began using misdemeanor charges such as disorderly conduct, vagrancy, lewdness, and loitering to harass gay men.[12] In 1923, the New York state legislature tailored its statutes to specify for the first time that a man's "frequent[ing] or loiter[ing] about any public place soliciting men for the purpose of committing a crime against nature or other lewdness" was punishable as a form of disorderly conduct.[13] Many more men were arrested and prosecuted under this misdemeanor charge than for the felony charge of sodomy, since misdemeanor laws carried fewer procedural protections for defendants. Between 1923 and 1966, when Mayor John Lindsay ordered the police to stop using entrapment by plainclothes officers to secure arrests of gay men, more than 50,000 men had been arrested on this charge in New York City alone.[14] The number of arrests escalated dramatically after the Second World War. More than 3,000 New Yorkers were arrested every year on this charge in the late 1940s. By 1950, Philadelphia's six-man "morals squad" was arresting more gay men than the courts knew how to handle, some 200 a month. In the District of Columbia, there were more than a thousand arrests every year.[15]

Fifty years ago, more than half of the nation's states, including New York, Michigan, and California, enacted laws authorizing the police to force persons who were convicted of certain sexual offenses, including sodomy—or, in some states, merely suspected of being "sexual deviants"—to undergo psychiatric examinations. Many of these laws authorized the indefinite confinement of homosexuals in mental institutions, from which they were to be released only if they were cured of their homosexuality, something prison doctors soon began to complain was impossible. The medical director of a state hospital in California argued that "Whenever a doubt arises in the judge's mind" that a suspect "might be a sexual deviate, maybe by his mannerisms or his dress, something to attract the attention, I think he should immediately call for a psychiatric examination." Detroit's prosecuting attorney demanded the authority to arrest, examine, and possibly confine indefinitely "anyone who exhibited abnormal sexual behavior, whether or not dangerous."[16]

Fifty years ago, in other words, homosexuals were not just ridiculed and scorned. They were systematically denied their civil rights: their right to free assembly, to patronize public accommodations, to free speech, to a free press, to a form of intimacy of their own choosing. And they confronted a degree of policing and harassment that is almost unimaginable to us today.

*T*HIS HISTORY of antigay discrimination is typically *mis-*remembered in at least two important ways.

First, this history is almost entirely forgotten. Even well-educated Americans are often startled to learn that the government dismissed more homosexuals than communists at the height of the McCarthy era. It's likely you were startled to learn that there was a legal ban on plays with lesbian or gay characters. But calling this a forgotten history is really too benign. It's more accurate to say this history of discrimination has been erased from the historical record, and that this erasure itself has been a central element of antigay politics. For a long time young historians were warned that pursuing research on such matters would destroy their careers. Even today, most history departments are reluctant to hire scholars whose research focuses on the gay past. Few private foundations or federal agencies consider funding gay research.

But we forget this history at our peril. The opponents of gay rights themselves remain ignorant of this history, and the success of their arguments often depends on the gay community's historical amnesia and on the larger public's ignorance about the history and current realities of gay lives. Erasing the history of antigay discrimination makes it easier to argue that gay people do not need or deserve the most basic civil rights protections. Erasing the history of gay political disfranchisement makes it easier to vilify gay people as a powerful, conspiratorial class whose struggle for full equality threatens the American dream instead of fulfilling it. And forgetting this history weakens the gay movement internally as well, because it cannot understand where it is today unless it understands how it got here.

But if this history has been forgotten, it has also been exaggerated. Gay people, as much as their opponents, tend to imagine that social hostility toward homosexuals is age-old and unchanging, and that ours is the first generation to live in relative freedom. It's not hard to understand why we think this. When the gay movement arose in the 1950s and 1960s, it confronted an array of discriminatory measures and attitudes so entrenched and powerful that it was easy to imagine they had always existed. But in fact they were an unprecedented and relatively short-lived development of the twentieth century.

The state and the church did have a long-standing interest in regulating sexual *behavior*—through constantly changing laws regulating marriage or prohibiting prostitution, bestiality, or sodomy. But the prohibition against sodomy was not the same thing as antigay discrimination. Since American colonial times various sodomy laws in various states criminalized a diverse and inconsistent set of nonprocreative sexual acts engaged in by diverse combinations of partners. Most sodomy laws applied equally to male–male, male–female, and human–animal sexual activity, and almost never to sexual relations between women. On the eve of the Civil War, none of the nation's sodomy laws penalized oral sex. In other words, "sodomy" as these statutes usually defined it was *not* the equivalent of homosexual conduct, which would have applied equally and exclusively to any kind of sexual contact between men and between women. More important, those laws regulated *conduct*—conduct in which *anyone* (or at least any male person) could engage. And they were rarely enforced before the late nineteenth century.[17]

Only in the twentieth century did the state begin to classify and discriminate against certain people on the basis of their sexual identity or *status* as homosexuals. Only in the twentieth century did the government and many Americans identify a category of people as outsiders to the nation, and even as its enemy, on the basis of their "sexual identity" alone. All of the discriminatory measures I've just described were put in place between the 1920s and 1950s, and most were dismantled between the 1960s and 1990s. Although such antigay discrimination is popularly thought to have ancient roots, in fact it is a unique and relatively short-lived product of the twentieth century.

How do we explain the rise and fall and persistence in anti-homosexual attitudes and discrimination in the twentieth century? We should never treat such animus as predictable or inevitable, or as a purely individual psychological phenomenon. To treat it in this way concedes the playing field to antigay bigotry before the battle has even begun, and makes it impossible to explain how attitudes change over time. Anti-homosexual sentiment is neither natural nor inevitable. We know this because of the remarkable growth in acceptance of gay people in our own time. But even in the past, American society has never been united in its hostility toward homosexuals. The growth of antigay hostility, as much as its decline, is a challenge for historical explanation.

As I showed in my book *Gay New York*, antigay attitudes were neither so virulent nor so universal in the early twentieth century as we retrospectively assume. The growing visibility of gay subcultures in American cities in the late nineteenth and early twentieth centuries was greeted by many people with fascination and intrigue. Popular images of "queers" focused on the "mannish women" and effeminate men who were, indeed, more prominent then on the streets and stages of the city than today, and gay men and lesbians often had to fight ridicule and harassment to claim their place. But many people regarded gay life as simply one more sign of the growing complexity and freedom from restrictive tradition of a burgeoning metropolitan culture. Gay and straight men casually interacted in the crowded streets, saloons, and speakeasies of the early twentieth-century city, and gay life was especially visible and accepted in working-class immigrant and African-American neighborhoods. Popular fascination with gay culture reached a crescendo during the Prohibition Era (or Jazz Age) of the 1920s, when lesbians ran some of the most popular tearooms and cafés in New York's Greenwich Village and Chicago's Towertown. Thousands of New Yorkers attended the drag balls organized by black gay men in Harlem in the 1920s and 1930s, and in 1931 two of the most successful nightclubs in Times Square featured openly gay entertainers.[18]

Even the antivice societies organized by Protestants in the late nineteenth century initially paid relatively little attention to the gay world. They regarded it as one more egregious sign of the loosening of social controls on sexual expression in cities dominated by Catholic and Jewish immigrants, but they devoted less attention to the suppression of gay life than to the suppression of immigrant saloons. They encouraged the police to step up harassment of gay life only as an incidental feature of their campaigns to shut down dance halls and movie theaters, prohibit the consumption of alcohol and the use of contraceptives, dissuade restaurants from serving an in-terracial mix of customers, and otherwise impose their vision of the proper social order and sexual morality on others—and they discovered there was no more consensus for the suppression of gay life than for alcohol.

Antivice activists were so much more concerned about prohibiting heterosexual than homosexual vice that they often passed up opportunities to police gay life. In 1928, for example, three antivice investigators arriving at a "Fag Masquerade Ball" in Harlem "found approximately 5,000 people, colored and white, men attired in women's clothes and vice versa," but they "shortly departed" after realizing they "could learn nothing" about female prostitution. Similarly, the churches devoted so much more effort to condemning illicit heterosexual than homosexual behavior and medical authorities warned so strenuously about the risk of contracting then-deadly venereal diseases from heterosexual contact that some men believed sexual contact with another man was less dangerous to their bodies and souls than sex with a woman.[19]

Others were more troubled by the growing visibility of lesbian and gay life, even though they usually regarded it as simply an unfortunate effect of more troubling trends like massive immigration, urban disorder, and, especially, women's challenge of restrictive gender roles. Much of the early hostility to homosexuals was motivated by the uneasiness many men felt about the dramatic changes underway in gender roles at the turn of the last century. Conservative physicians initially argued that the homosexual (or "sexual invert") was characterized as much by his or her violation of conventional gender roles as by specifically sexual interests. At a time when many doctors argued that women should be barred from most jobs because they thought employment would damage their ability to bear children, numerous doctors identified women's challenges to the limits placed on their sex as clinical evidence of a medical disorder. Thus doctors explained around 1900 that "the female possessed of masculine ideas of independence" was a "degenerate" and that "a decided taste and tolerance for cigars . . . [the] dislike and incapacity for needlework . . . and some capacity for athletics" were all signs of female "sexual inversion."[20] Similarly, another doctor thought it significant that a male "pervert" had "never smoked and never married; [and] was entirely averse to outdoor games."[21]

Such "scientific" views about sexual inversion lost their credibility once public opinion came to accept significant changes in women's roles in the workplace and politics, but doctors continued for several decades to identify homosexuality itself as a "disease," "mental defect," "disorder," or "degeneration." This shift in focus occurred as the stature of medical (and especially psychological and psychoanalytic) opinion grew in American society. The medical profession had limited influence in the late nineteenth century, and reached its peak of influence in the decades following the Second World War. Especially from the onset of the war until the American Psychiatric Association removed homosexuality from its list of disorders in 1973, such hostile medical pronouncements would provide a powerful source of legitimation to antihomosexual sentiment, much as medical science had previously legitimized widely held (and subsequently discarded) beliefs about male superiority and white racial superiority.[22]

Although medical warnings about homosexuality prolifer-
ated in the early twentieth century, the state and other disci-
plinary authorities did not begin to focus significant attention
on homosexuality until the 1930s. The vigor and popularity of
their efforts resulted in part from the Great Depression,
which many Americans blamed on the cultural experimentation and moral "excesses" of the Jazz Age, of which the élan of
gay culture seemed an especially egregious example. But the
gender upheavals of the 1930s played a more decisive role in
generating antigay hostility. By depriving millions of men of
their role as breadwinners, the Depression precipitated a massive crisis in gender and family relations. Public work projects
and other programs were designed to restore men's status in
their families and larger society, even when this meant limit-
ing women's economic opportunities. The fragility of the
gender order made the visibility of gay life seem more threatening given the long-standing representation of queers as
gender deviants. After a generation in which gay life had been
highly visible and relatively integrated into urban public life,
it was forced into hiding by the new laws that pushed gay people out of restaurants and bars and off the stage.[23]

Hostility toward homosexuals only increased in the anxious
years following the Second World War, when communists,
criminal syndicates, and other half-invisible specters seemed
to threaten the nation and when demonic new stereotypes of
homosexuals were created and backed by government sanction. Homosexuals were not thought to be communists, as
some have since imagined. Rather, homosexuals were depicted
in ways that drew on patterns of demonization that had become familiar and habitual through their widespread use to

demonize Jews as well as communists. The old tropes of anti-Semitic rhetoric (which the Holocaust had made less respectable though hardly erased) were especially influential in shaping depictions of homosexuals. Thus lesbians and gay men were increasingly denounced as cosmopolitan outsiders whose loyalties were not to the nation but to an international or extranational community of people like themselves. Some congressmen and magazines claimed they constituted a "Homintern" (a term playing on the Comintern, or Communist International), which controlled Broadway, Hollywood, and other media, and used their immense cultural power to undermine American values.[24] In an era when fears of political and criminal conspiracy were especially powerful, homosexuals were depicted as part of a formidable and invisible conspiracy that threatened American culture. And like Jews, they were depicted as a threat to children.

In the most dangerous element of this new image, the escalation of antigay policing was accompanied, inspired, and justified by press and police campaigns that fomented stereotypes of homosexuals as child molesters. Several brutal but isolated sexual attacks on children prompted a series of nationwide campaigns that depicted the country as overrun by murderous sex deviates. Most of the children attacked by men were girls, and many knew their assailants. But the press campaigns claimed instead that strangers and above all homosexuals were the primary threats to children, warning that by engaging in homosexual behavior, a man had demonstrated the refusal to adjust to social norms that was the hallmark of the psychopath. One popular magazine asserted in 1950, for instance, that "Once a man assumes the role of homosexual, he often throws off all moral restraints. . . . Some male sex deviants do not stop with infecting their often-innocent partners: they descend through perversions to other forms of depravity, such as drug addiction, burglary, sadism, and even murder." The male homosexual had long been regarded as a sissy-man, whom one might ridicule but had no reason to fear. Now he came to be seen as an inveterate child molestor, predator, and psychopath.[25]

Government leaders joined the press in portraying homosexuals as part of a conspiracy that threatened the nation's security as well as its children. In 1950, following Senator Joseph McCarthy's denunciation of the employment of homosexuals in the State Department, the Senate conducted a special investigation into "the employment of homosexuals and other sex perverts in government." The Senate Committee's report gave the national government's imprimatur to antigay bigotry when it recommended excluding gay men and lesbians from government service because they were criminals, predators, and "security risks," who "lack[ed] the emotional stability of normal persons." "Government officials have the responsibility of keeping this type of corrosive influence out of the agencies under their control," the Committee warned. "One homosexual can pollute a Government office."[26]

Two years after the Senate Committee recommended that homosexuals be purged from government employment, the Congress as a whole signaled its conviction that homosexuals stood outside the boundaries of the nation in the most palpable way possible: by denying them entry to the country. Congress has always defined its vision of the ideal national community by identifying those who would *not* be allowed to join it. It defined the nation in racial terms in its first naturalization law, passed in 1790, which made citizenship available only to immigrants who were "free white persons," and in laws enacted between the 1880s and 1920s that prohibited most Asians from entering the country. In the 1920s, when the massive immigration of Catholics and Jews from southern and eastern Europe threatened the nation's self-definition as an Anglo-Saxon Protestant society, Congress severely restricted such immigration. And in 1952, when many American leaders held up the heterosexual, suburban, nuclear family as a fundamental emblem and safeguard of the American way of life, the Congress prohibited homosexuals (whom it called psychopaths) as well as communists from entering the country. A generation of foreign visitors applying for tourist visas had to sign statements swearing they belonged to neither one of these threatening groups, and a generation of lesbian and gay male immigrants were compelled to hide their identities from the authorities. Yet the real-life consequences of this exclusion of homosexuals from the nation did not stop there. Even lesbians and gay men who were American citizens found themselves virtually stripped of their civil rights.

WE CONTINUE TO LIVE WITH the legacy of the antigay measures enacted in the 1930s, 1940s, and 1950s, in the discriminatory laws still on the books and in the popular hostility such laws expressed, perpetuated, and legitimized. Such forms of discrimination and harassment were so pervasive and well established by the 1960s that it was widely imagined they were the inevitable residue of an age-old, unchanging social antipathy toward homosexuality. But despite their seeming timelessness and inevitability, most such forms of discrimination are of recent origin and short duration.

We likewise witness all about us the continuing power of the stereotype of the homosexual as child molester. It remains potent enough to incite and justify widespread opposition to gay rights, particularly the rights of gay teachers, parents, and couples wishing to marry, and its nearly elemental force makes it easy to imagine that it is a timeless image. But anti-gay stereotypes, like the anti-Semitic and racist stereotypes with which they have much in common, are historically variable, and this one is primarily a creation of the postwar period.

Antigay animus is not an artifact of human nature but a product of human history. Public attitudes and state policies changed to become more hostile in mid–twentieth-century America. Over the next several decades, they changed again. After being forced to hide, lesbians and gay men reentered the public sphere to fight the new forms of discrimination. As a result, the life experiences and popular images of gay people changed once more, although old fears fueled strong resistance to that change. The marriage debate at the end of the twentieth century exploded at the confluence of these historical trends.

TWO

Gay Rights, Civil Rights

*H*ow did we get from the world of pervasive antigay discrimination just fifty years ago to a world in which a conservative Catholic Supreme Court justice like Anthony Kennedy could declare that such discrimination is antithetical to our nation's principles? How did we get from the San Francisco of 1960, where the mayor launched a sustained crackdown on gay bars, to the San Francisco of 2004, where the mayor issued thousands of marriage licenses to same-sex couples? How did the situation of lesbians and gay men change so much in so little time?

None of this change was inevitable, just as none of it is irreversible. It depended on the emergence after the Second World War of a gay "identity movement" set in motion by the relentless assertion by the state and other authorities that sexual identity provided a key to the self and that being gay categorically barred one from citizenship rights. The success of that movement ultimately depended on the willingness of hundreds of thousands of people to risk their jobs, reputations, and ties to their families by joining together to change the conditions of their lives.

But the changing place of lesbians and gay men also de-

pended on broader changes in American society and the nation's expanding vision of civil rights. The story of the profound transformation in gay life is not just a queer history,
taking its own singular shape outside of the main currents of
American history. It was instead deeply bound up in the
broader social transformations of the last half century, from
the changing status of women to the changing cultural politics of race and ethnicity. Above all, the gay movement, like
every other postwar movement for minority rights and social
justice, was profoundly influenced by the powerful model of
the black civil rights movement.

Postwar Gay Culture and Politics

The dramatic escalation in the policing of gay life after the
Second World War did not eradicate it. In most cities, lesbians
and gay men continued to keep up an active gay social life.
They patronized gay bars and bathhouses, turned various
nightclubs and restaurants into their informal meeting places,
and packed Carnegie Hall to hear Judy Garland sing their
songs. They took over remote sections of public beaches and
held dances in the ballrooms of Harlem lodges. When the police shut down a favorite bar, they moved to another. When
police crackdowns were especially severe—and even when
they weren't—people threw open their homes for gay parties.
They read Gore Vidal's *The City and the Pillar*, James Baldwin's
Giovanni's Room, and other postwar novels with gay themes,
Ann Bannon's many tales of lesbian life and love, and a steady
stream of lesbian "pulp" novels. As theater censorship waned,

they saw some of the decade's most talked-about plays—Tennessee Williams' *Cat on a Hot Tin Roof* and Robert Anderson's *Tea and Sympathy*—turn "homosexual themes" into "universal" themes. (Such themes still had to be erased or remain heavily coded when the plays were adapted for the big screen.) In many smaller towns, gay life took shape unnoticed in church choirs, amateur theaters, and women's softball leagues and was sustained by closely knit social circles and a ceaseless round of parties. In rural Ohio one farmer threw huge gay dances in his barn. In urban working-class neighborhoods, lesbian butches walked down the streets wearing men's trousers and slicked back hair, daring anyone to stop them.[1]

Most people responded to the escalation in policing after the Second World War by remaining more hidden than did the butches and queens. But they developed elaborate verbal codes that allowed them to communicate with one another while remaining invisible to hostile outsiders. The word *gay* is a good example of this, since before the 1970s few heterosexuals realized gay people had given it a distinctly homosexual meaning. One lesbian could tell another at a crowded office party that she was leaving for a gay party or to have a gay time with some friends without bystanders having a clue what she meant. The very success of such subterfuges in concealing the gay world meant that it was more difficult for people to find gay life in the 1950s than it is today. Many remained isolated and unsure of themselves as a result. But when they found the gay world, most people discovered it to be larger and more welcoming than they ever could have imagined.

Most gay people conducted themselves according to the terms of an unofficial and unacknowledged moral accord with their families and the authorities, which led them to feel relatively (but never entirely) secure so long as they did nothing to draw attention to themselves. Long before the military formalized the rule in 1993, an informal policy of "Don't ask, don't tell" governed gay life. So long as gay people remained "discreet" and didn't tell people they were gay, most of their fellow workers and straight friends did not care to ask. Some gay people found it stressful to live a double life and difficult to keep their gay and straight social worlds separate, but given the draconian new laws of the postwar period, they simply had no choice. Indeed, to a degree that is difficult to grasp today, most gay people became extraordinarily adept at—and habituated to—doing so. Many even resented and avoided the drag queens, "sissy men," and butch lesbians who refused to conform publicly, sometimes blaming them for drawing attention to the gay world.

Much of the earliest gay organizing was motivated by the perception that the state had violated the terms of this unwritten accord through its increasingly intrusive surveillance and policing of gay life. Thousands of homosexuals who had risked their lives in the Second World War were identified and dishonorably discharged from the armed forces, especially near the end of hostilities when their manpower was less needed, which prompted small bands of them to protest to the government. After the war, even people who abided by the conventions of discretion ran increased risks of being arrested in raids on bars and private parties, of being caught when it turned out a man they'd met at a bar was a plainclothes policeman, or losing their jobs because they had been identified and tracked down by the surveillance apparatus of the state or federal government. Frank Kameny, for one, might have continued to balance his government career as an astronomer with an active gay life. But after he was dismissed for being homosexual in 1957, he founded the first gay rights group in Washington, D.C., and devoted his life to fighting government discrimination. Long before masses of gay people chose to come out of the closet, the national government itself played a crucial role in destroying the walls between people's "public" roles as workers and churchgoers and their "private" lives as homosexuals.[2]

The earliest movement organizations faced formidable odds. The Mattachine Society and Daughters of Bilitis were founded in the early 1950s at the height of the demonization of homosexuals as dangerous, irrational, and unstable pariahs who threatened the nation's children as well as national security. They were deeply influenced by the way other marginalized groups framed their case and challenged the myths used to justify their stigmatization. No political program enjoyed universal support within the movement, but three elements were especially important.[3]

First, many activists embraced the rights discourse and concern with minorities that had acquired renewed cultural force in the 1940s and 1950s. The government had rallied support for the Second World War by portraying it as a war in defense of freedom and minority rights against Nazi racism and Japanese imperialism, and then had played a leading role in developing the Universal Declaration of Human Rights adopted by the United Nations in 1948. Following the war, the mass mobilization of ordinary African-Americans—sharecroppers and maids, students and clergy—to secure their freedom and the entrenched opposition they faced moved the question of civil rights to the center of the national agenda. Many lesbians and gay men already shared a strong group consciousness, and some activists embraced the new political language to portray themselves as a rights-bearing *minority* of American *citizens* rather than as subversive *aliens* from a psychopathic and criminal underworld. In 1951, one of the earliest leaders of the gay movement, Donald Webster Cory, published his influential book *The Homosexual in America*, which began by noting the growing attention being paid to the question of minority rights—and then boldly suggesting that homosexuals constituted a minority group that deserved its rights like any other.

Second, the initial generation of activists worked to educate and cultivate allies among sociologists, psychologists, criminologists, and other professionals who had the credibility to speak on homosexuality that was denied homosexuals themselves. No lawmaker would grant a homosexual a hearing in the 1950s, but activists hoped that professional authorities could be persuaded to reevaluate their images of homosexual pathology and then would, in turn, help persuade lawmakers and the public. One of the first such advances came when a group of gay men in Los Angeles persuaded the psychologist Evelyn Hooker to conduct a study of them. The resulting article was one of the first to be based on a group of homosexuals not seeking treatment for mental distress; not surprisingly, it was also among the first to find that not all homosexuals suffered from mental illness.

Third, like the leaders of many minority and ethnic groups in the 1950s, the nascent gay movement embraced a largely assimilationist platform by stressing their allegiance to the nation, their desire to integrate the homosexual into the larger society, their conformity with all American social conventions save the one that distinguished them, and their desire to restrain the public behavior of other homosexuals who did not share their assimilationist intentions. The very term they used for their movement—homophile—was designed to minimize the source of their difference from "normal Americans": their homosexual desire.

But in the 1960s and 1970s, the gay movement broke decisively with the assimilationist rhetoric of the 1950s by publicly affirming, celebrating, and even cultivating homosexual difference.[4] In doing so, it was deeply influenced by the growth of black cultural nationalism, which rejected assimilation in favor of encouraging pride in black cultural difference. Its influence could be seen everywhere in the gay movement. When a conference of gay activists formally adopted the slogan *Gay is Good* in 1968, after considerable debate, they were directly inspired by the growing African-American insistence that *Black is Beautiful*. The decision in 1970 to call the first anniversary march commemorating the resistance that greeted a police raid on the Stonewall bar in June 1969 a *Gay Pride March*, and, indeed, the whole focus since then on developing self-acceptance and pride in people who were ashamed of being gay, was directly inspired by the earlier movement to instill *Black Pride*. The long term effort to build an affirmative gay culture—including gay theater, films, music, and newspapers—was also influenced by the Black Arts movement, Chicano mural movement, and other grassroots ethnic cultural movements seeking to foster community solidarity and pride in cultural difference.

This generational change in consciousness was advanced by the emergence of the gay liberation movement at the end of the decade. Organized by young gay people who often had more experience in the civil rights movement, the New Left, feminism, and antiwar protests than in the gay world, it was deeply influenced by the tactics, organizational forms, and aspirations of those movements. Inspired by the rioting that began after the police tried to arrest the patrons of the Stonewall Bar, including many people of color, hustlers, and drag queens, the gay liberationists organized an extraordinary range of new organizations. Collectively, they broke decisively with the old patterns of gay life in three important ways.

First, lesbian and gay liberationists were deeply influenced by the rebirth of feminism. By encouraging people to think critically about the sex roles that structured relations between men and women and limited women's choices in life, work, and love, feminism gave gay male and especially lesbian liberationists a framework for analyzing their oppression. Although the role of lesbians in the women's movement remained internally contested, many lesbian activists came to identify with the women's movement more than with the mostly male-led gay movement, and lesbian and gay activists often had contentious relations. The growing influence of the feminist critique of sex roles and the concrete achievements of the women's movement nonetheless provided an important impetus to the development of both lesbian and gay politics and provided a wider base of support for their critique of heterosexual superiority. But the links between the two movements also inspired fear and resentment on the part of many others, and would shape feminist and gay politics into the next century.

Second, many activists devoted themselves to transforming the old gay world (which they now perceived to be as alienating, fragmenting, and objectifying as the larger society they criticized) into a more humane, organic, and, ironically, self-segregating gay community. Lesbians played a major role in the creation of an extensive "women's community" or "women's culture" of feminist bookstores, coffeeshops, newspapers, poetry readings, and music festivals, which played a key role in sustaining feminist politics. The efforts of men and women alike resulted in the creation of a vastly expanded and more cohesive gay community. There had been fewer than fifty gay organizations in the country on the eve of Stonewall; by 1974, there were almost a thousand. Activists started gay newspapers, bookstores, radio shows, film festivals, college groups, communes, music festivals, record companies, churches, and community centers. They also established gay caucuses in unions, professional organizations, academic societies, and churches, as well as a host of all-purpose gay liberation and civil rights organizations. If gay men had once socialized covertly in church choirs, now they established Gay Men's Choruses that mixed show-tunes with the gospels. If lesbians had once met in company and neighborhood softball teams, now they established lesbian and gay sports leagues and a gay version of the Olympics.

Many of the organizations were inspired by comparable organizations founded by other minority movements. When the Lambda Legal Defense and Education Fund was established in 1973, it modeled itself on the NAACP Legal Defense and

Education Fund. The older group had waged a brilliant campaign under the leadership of Thurgood Marshall to dismantle segregation. *Brown v. Board of Education* was its most famous victory. The gay movement's later legal victories in the Supreme Court over political disfranchisement in *Romer v. Evans* and over sodomy laws in *Lawrence v. Texas* both depended on the success of the NAACP in reviving the Fourteenth Amendment's guarantees of substantive due process and equal protection. Similarly, when the Gay and Lesbian Alliance Against Defamation (or GLAAD) was established in 1985, it modeled itself on the B'nai B'rith Anti-Defamation League. Since then, GLAAD's considerable success in changing and diversifying the representation of LGBT people in the media has relied in no small part on the earlier successes of Jewish, black, and feminist groups in sensitizing the media to the civic responsibilities that come with their considerable power to influence the national dialogue on social and ethical issues.

The third and most decisive way the gay liberation movement broke with earlier convention was to insist on the importance of gay people "coming out" to heterosexuals. Coming out of the closet, to use the now familiar phrase that appeared only in the 1960s, was deemed to be an act crucial both to personal liberation and to the emancipation of other, closeted homosexuals—in part by rendering visible one's homosexual difference, in part by normalizing homosexuality by showing outsiders that homosexuals were not so different from them and that anyone, not just "obvious" drag queens and butch lesbians, might be one.

But even the decision to come out, a development sometimes regarded as uniquely gay, was bound up in the larger transformations of the 1960s and 1970s. It was inspired by the general democratization of American society, which included a wide-ranging challenge to the patterns of discretion and deference that had served to reinforce social hierarchies. The most famous and influential example of this came when massive numbers of African-Americans in the South risked and suffered violent retribution by disrupting the long-established rules of etiquette that had sustained white supremacy. Many black youth, in particular, refused any longer to keep their dissatisfaction to themselves or to pretend they accepted their subordination ("their place") by stepping off the sidewalk to let white people pass, doffing their hats to them, drinking at "colored" water fountains, and in general remaining silent. Instead they began to directly challenge their subordination, in their everyday interactions with whites as well as in their mass mobilizations.

In this social context, coming out to heterosexuals became a new moral imperative, an existentialist act of witness to the truth of oneself that became even more compelling at a time when many social movements called on people to engage in such risky acts of witness, from sitting at a segregated lunch counter to burning a draft card. The cultural power of the quest for authenticity and personal wholeness in the late 1960s and 1970s also helped spark this campaign for self-transformation and self-revelation, and gave it enduring force. But the impetus to come out was influenced as well by the so-called ethnic revival of the 1970s. In proclaiming and even cultivating their sense of difference from the national norm, gay people followed the lead of African-Americans,

Chicanos, Jews, Italians, and others who were also embracing differences they had once downplayed or concealed.[5]

The movement to come out was also profoundly shaped by the sexual revolution. Throughout the industrialized world, the mid-1960s through the 1970s marked an epochal shift in sexual behavior and norms. It became common for couples to live together before getting married, or even with no intention of getting married. Divorce rates skyrocketted. The wide availability of the birth control pill made it easier for people to have sex without fear of pregnancy and encouraged the acceptance of sexual relations as a source of pleasure and form of communication that did not need to be justified by reproductive intentions. These developments made lesbians, bisexuals, and gay men bolder and more confident. All around them, they saw their heterosexual friends decisively rejecting the moral codes of their parents's generation, which had limited sex to marriage, and forging a new moral code that linked sex to love and common consent. The fact that so many young heterosexuals considered sexual freedom to be a marker of personal freedom made lesbians and gay men feel their quest for freedom was part of a larger movement. The fact that so many in their generation insisted on frankness in sexual matters encouraged lesbians and gay men to be openly gay. The mass decision to come out was encouraged by the sexual revolution and eventually became one of its most enduring symbols.

Over the next thirty years, the mass movement to come out succeeded in humanizing lesbians and gay men for many outsiders, making the demonization of homosexuals less persuasive and less acceptable, and rallying many heterosexuals to support the rights of people they now realized were not alien pariahs but often among those they most loved and respected. But it also frightened many other outsiders, disrupted engrained patterns of accommodation for gay and straight people alike, and initially made gay people even more vulnerable to discrimination. Above all, gay people's new openness and insistence on their equality with heterosexuals soon made gay freedom a primary target of the growing movement to reimpose "traditional family values" of all sorts. This conflict would ultimately move the civil rights of gay people to the center of national debate.

New Openings in the 1970s

Although gay liberation challenged the rhetoric of the pre-Stonewall movement, gay liberationists shared many of its goals: ending the police harassment of gay spaces (such as bars and dance clubs); ending the stigmatization of homosexuality by cultural authorities (doctors, clergy, and government officials); and ending discrimination in employment and other arenas.[6]

The most significant early victories of the movement curtailed the police harassment of gay life. With some striking exceptions, this victory is by now so nearly complete that it is almost forgotten. But it would be hard to overstate its magnitude. The New York Mattachine Society's success in 1966 in forcing Mayor John Lindsay to end the widespread police use of entrapment had a profound effect on gay male New Yorkers, who for the first time in decades did not have to worry that the men who came on to them in bars and elsewhere were undercover cops. Throughout the country, a combination of political actions, court rulings that homosexuals had to be allowed to hold hands, dance, or do anything else heterosexuals did in bars, and the general decline in the policing of urban nightlife all played a role in reducing the harassment of gay gathering places. Still, the pace of change was uneven.

In some cities, such as New York and San Francisco, court rulings and political mobilization brought an end to widespread harassment in the mid-1960s, before the birth of gay liberation. (The famous raid on the Stonewall bar in 1969 was more anomalous then, and thus more provocative, than it would have been just five years earlier.) But in many other cities, the police continued to raid bars with impunity well into the 1970s. The decriminalization of gay businesses in some cities led to a proliferation of gay bars and dance clubs. In the 1970s, this turned San Francisco, New York, and a handful of other cities into burgeoning gay meccas, fostered a new sexual ethics, and encouraged the massive migration of gay men and women from other parts of the country. An alternative, less commercialized lesbian feminist community took shape in some college towns as well as major cities. But the burgeoning commercial world of dance clubs and bars won the allegiance of many young gay men and ironically drew them away from participation in the movement itself, even as they also fostered a sense of community identification that the movement could later tap.

Activists parlayed the general liberalization of the 1960s and 1970s into several other early victories. Most strikingly, gay activists working in concert with doctors and social scientists who had conducted research on homosexuality were able to persuade some of the major institutions that had long helped legitimize antigay attitudes to change their positions. Medical writers and mental health professionals were among the first to change their views. In 1973, the American Psychiatric Association voted to remove homosexuality from its list of mental disorders.[7] The American Psychological Association and the American Medical Association soon followed suit.[8]

Religious attitudes toward homosexuals and homosexuality also began to change. The debate in the churches over the place of lesbians and gay men in religious life would sharpen in the following decades, but in the 1970s many mainline Protestant denominations issued official statements condemning legal discrimination against homosexuals and affirming that homosexuals ought to enjoy equal protection under criminal and civil law. Several of these groups descended from the historically influential denominations whose religious authority had been invoked to justify colonial sodomy statutes and the policing of homosexuality as one more sign of urban vice. The Lutheran Church in America, the Unitarian Universalist Association, the United Methodist Church, the United Church of Christ, the Protestant Episcopal Church, the Disciples of Christ, and the United Presbyterian Church in the U.S.A. all issued statements in support of gay rights before 1980.[9] Many clergy offered their support by making their churches available for gay meetings. The Unitarians, Quakers, and Methodists were especially known for this, but even some Catholic priests allowed the new gay Catholic group, Dignity, to meet in parish facilities before the hierarchy forbade it.

The movement also succeeded in ending some forms of employment discrimination. In 1975, the U.S. Civil Service

Commission, which Frank Kameny had first challenged eighteen years earlier, lifted its ban on the employment of gay men and lesbians.[10] That same year, *Time* became the first major newsweekly ever to put a gay man on the cover: Leonard Matlovich, a decorated Vietnam veteran, who had been discharged for homosexuality and decided to fight it. He didn't win his case, but the unprecedented publicity his case received at least succeeded in introducing the idea that his dismissal should be seen as a form of discrimination.

The dramatic mobilization of lesbians and gay men in the 1970s set the stage for the earliest legislative victories, but they also depended on the continuing strength of a broader public commitment to civil rights. In 1972, East Lansing, Michigan, home to Michigan State University, became the first municipality to pass a gay rights ordinance. Within five years, twenty-eight communities had passed such legislation, more than half of them university towns such as Ann Arbor, Austin, Berkeley, and Madison. They were joined by a handful of larger cities with strong civil rights traditions, such as San Francisco, Minneapolis, Seattle, and Detroit. The ordinances typically amended antidiscrimination laws by simply adding sexual orientation to the list of grounds such as race, religion, and marital status that could not serve as grounds for discrimination, often only in employment. They effectively recognized homosexuals as a minority. Few of the first ordinances faced well-organized opposition.[11]

That changed in 1977, when the Baptist singer and Florida citrus growers' spokeswoman Anita Bryant led a campaign to "Save Our Children" from a newly enacted gay civil rights ordinance in Dade County, Florida. Her success in persuading a decisive majority of Miami voters to vote against the ordinance depended heavily on her use of the still powerful postwar images of homosexuals as child molesters. Dismissing the idea that homosexuals were a minority like any other, her organization ran a full-page newspaper ad the day before the vote warning that "The other side of the homosexual coin is a hair-raising pattern of recruitment and outright seductions and molestation."[12] Her victory prompted conservative groups in other cities to take up the cause, and in the next three years gay rights laws were struck down in more than half a dozen bitterly fought referenda stretching from St. Paul, Minnesota, to Eugene, Oregon. Gay rights advocates managed to stave off the assault only twice, in November 1978, when Seattle voted to preserve its antidiscrimination ordinance and California rejected the Briggs Initiative, a proposal so onerous—it would have prohibited public school teachers, gay or straight, from saying anything that could be construed as "advocating homosexuality"—that even former governor Ronald Reagan spoke out against it.[13] But no one had time to savor the victory over Briggs. Three weeks later, Harvey Milk, the first openly gay San Francisco city supervisor and one of the victory's chief architects, was assassinated.

The movement's early victories and the dramatic growth in gay organizations in the 1970s should not be overstated. The movement remained concentrated in certain cities and regions, had few genuinely national organizations, and had not yet entered the national stage of political and moral debate. Its weakness and the tenuous place of lesbians and gay men in American society became all too clear in the early 1980s. The conservative backlash against the growth of gay visibility, as well as against feminism and the civil rights movements of people of color, was visible not only in the Dade County vote but in the establishment of Jerry Falwell's Moral Majority and other conservative evangelical organizations in the late 1970s. In 1980, the country's growing right-wing movement contributed to Ronald Reagan's landslide election as president on a platform stressing "traditional family values."

From the gay perspective, his election could not have come at a worse time. For during the first year of his administration, a mysterious new disease was noticed that would change gay life forever.

AIDS, Retrenchment, and Resurgence in the 1980s and Early 1990s

The enduring conviction that homosexuals stood outside the moral boundaries of the nation profoundly shaped the earliest responses to AIDS in the United States. Even after the word AIDS (Acquired Immune Deficiency Syndrome) replaced the initial moniker GRID (Gay-Related Immune Deficiency), the syndrome was depicted as a disease that affected only homosexuals and Haitians, another group whose immigration and citizenship rights were being hotly contested.[14]

Media reports initially minimized the crisis by reassuring Americans that the nation—the "general public"—was not at risk. But the media "discovered" AIDS in 1985, when word got out that it had brought the actor Rock Hudson, one of the great heterosexual heartthrobs of the fifties, to the verge of death. The ensuing avalanche of sensationalist attention reinforced the image of homosexuals as dangerous outsiders who threatened the nation: diseased and dangerously hard to detect. Fear of contagion prompted a new wave of discrimination against gay people in medical care, housing, and employment. Even in cosmopolitan cities like New York, many heterosexuals became afraid to use the same phones or water fountains that gay men used, and in a handful of smaller cities, protests by parents forced schools to expel children with AIDS. The conservative writer William Buckley even proposed tattooing people with AIDS to make it impossible for them to circulate among the public unrecognized.

At the same time, the health crisis rapidly consuming the gay male community seemed so marginal and insignificant to the national interest that federal authorities refused to acknowledge it as a medical and national crisis. President Reagan did not even utter the word "AIDS" in public until his friend Rock Hudson became ill, and did not give a speech addressing the epidemic until six years had passed and 20,000 Americans had died.

But AIDS also led to an unprecedented mobilization of gay men and an equally unprecedented degree of cooperation between them and the large number of lesbians who played leading roles in the response to AIDS. In the face of the government's murderous neglect, gay activists launched an impressive array of new grassroots organizations to meet the urgent needs of people with AIDS. In January 1982, following the first reports of a strange new cancer affecting gay men, the playwright Larry Kramer and several other men founded Gay Men's Health Crisis in New York. Within months, like-minded activists in California founded the organizations that would ultimately be known as the San Francisco AIDS Foundation and the AIDS Project Los Angeles. They mobilized thousands of gay volunteers to serve as "buddies" to people with AIDS, cook their meals, clean their homes, and strenuously intervene on their behalf with doctors and other hospital personnel who were often as ignorant and frightened of the disease as laypeople were. They produced the leaflets, booklets, newspaper columns, and posters that, for a long time, were the only reliable source of information for a community desperate to sort out fact from frightened fantasy. Lesbians who had been involved in the women's health movement brought their sophisticated understanding of health care issues to fledgling AIDS organizations. The rapid expansion of existing organizations and the creation of new ones were extraordinary, but the very need for them reflected the government's refusal to take a "homosexual disease" seriously, and reinforced the gay community's recognition that the "general public" did not care about the health crisis surging through their community.

The growing anger many gay people felt erupted in 1986, when the Supreme Court upheld the nation's sodomy laws in *Bowers v. Hardwick*, using language that belittled the very idea that homosexuals had "a fundamental right . . . to engage in sodomy" as "facetious." The ruling put a roadblock in the way of gay rights litigation and emboldened the opponents of gay rights. Many lower courts interpreted the ruling to mean that discrimination against homosexuals was constitutionally permissible. Just as important, the sodomy laws' criminalization of homosexual activity served the larger ideological purpose of criminalizing all lesbians and gay men. *Bowers* gave the opponents of gay rights carte blanche to use this imputation of criminality to justify everything from excluding gays from the military to removing children from the homes of lesbian mothers. The APA had stopped calling homosexuals mentally ill in 1973; but in 1986, the Supreme Court effectively announced that they could still be called criminals.[15]

The effects on public opinion were dramatic. In 1987, six years after the Reagan administration came into office, six years after AIDS unleashed a new wave of fear of homosexuals, and one year after the *Bowers* decision, public disapproval of homosexuality reached its peak. Polling data showed virtually no change through the 1970s, but the number of people who declared that homosexual relations were always wrong climbed from 73 percent in 1980 to 78 percent in 1987.[16]

As the attacks on homosexuals escalated as rapidly as the death toll, people's shock and grief turned to anger and determination. Three thousand protestors filled the streets of New York the day *Bowers* was announced, and the following year a national march in Washington for lesbian, gay, bisexual, and transgender rights drew half a million. A new generation of militant activism was launched the same year with the founding of ACT UP (the AIDS Coalition to Unleash Power), a grassroots organization that orchestrated highly theatrical and media-savvy attacks on the institutions and individuals they held responsible for the status quo: political officials who pretended the disease did not affect their constituents, public health agencies that acted as if AIDS was not a threat to "public" health, and drug companies that thought they could gouge a stigmatized and defenseless group of people with unconscionably high prices. ACT UP shut down Wall Street, unfurled huge AIDS banners at Yankee Stadium, invaded the campus of the National Institutes of Health, and plastered the streets with posters warning that *Silence=Death*. A new generation took that message to heart. The growing recognition that public attitudes and government policies toward homosexuals carried literally life or death consequences led many people who had found a comfortable niche for themselves to end their silence, as complacency began to feel like complicity.[17]

The AIDS movement also reinvigorated many older organizations and mobilized a new generation of activists who took up gay issues in many arenas. Lambda Legal and other older groups hired more staff as they benefited from an infusion of new support and donations. Queer Nation took the feisty politics of ACT UP into suburban shopping malls. GLAAD, the Gay and Lesbian Alliance Against Defamation, founded in 1985 to challenge the demonization of homosexuals as immoral purveyors of disease, mobilized hundreds of people to protest the most egregious stories and put the press on notice that it could no longer defame homosexuals with impunity.

Their efforts and the new openness and assertiveness of gay journalists prompted soul-searching and debate in many of the nation's newsrooms, which contributed to the media developing a more complex portrait of the AIDS crisis. The press began paying more attention to the gay community's mobilization in response to the epidemic. In the course of giving the epidemic a human face, it often told stories about gay couples, "buddies," and support groups that communicated the complexity and humanity of gay people's lives to millions.

The spread of AIDS and the steady escalation of gay issues at the local level fueled a growing polarization of the nation in the 1980s. This can be seen in the fate of local gay rights ordinances, which became an important barometer of public attitudes toward homosexuality as well as of the relative strength of pro- and antigay forces. Increased gay political mobilization and changing attitudes allowed activists to secure the enactment of gay rights ordinances in another forty cities, counties, and suburbs, including New York, Chicago, and Atlanta, bringing the national total to eighty. But these victories were often more difficult to achieve than they had been in the 1970s. In New York City, for instance, where the law passed the city council only after more than a decade of struggle, gay activists faced the combined opposition of the Catholic archbishop, Orthodox Jews, and evangelical Protestants.[18]

Groups that had already managed to pass gay rights laws found them under attack from an increasingly well-organized and well-funded right wing. Beginning in 1988 and reaching a crescendo in 1992–1994, right-wing groups in Colorado, Oregon, Maine, and half a dozen other states used antigay referendum initiatives to build local organizations based on networks of conservative churches, which were quick to coordinate efforts with right-wing groups in other states. Gay groups were thrown on the defensive in some areas and barely existed in others. They hastily formed local and statewide organizations, some of which became an enduring presence in their states, and they often managed to mobilize legions of dedicated volunteers to mount a strong response to antigay campaigns. The National Gay and Lesbian Task Force began offering training and support to local activists. But the thin networks of gay newspapers, bookstores, and social and political organizations existing in most areas were little match for the Christian Right's juggernaut of radio stations, cable and television programs, extensive church networks, and national coordinating organizations. In the twenty years after Anita Bryant's campaign in Miami, gay activists faced more than sixty antigay rights referenda around the country. In Oregon alone, there were sixteen local antigay initiatives in 1993 and another eleven in 1994; gay activists lost all but one. Nationwide, gay rights supporters lost almost three-quarters of them.[19]

The referendum campaigns were especially dangerous to the gay movement because antigay groups used them to reframe the gay rights debate by claiming homosexuals were not seeking "equal protection" or "equal rights" but "*special* rights." One of the main antigay groups in Oregon even named itself the No Special Rights Committee. A generation earlier, conservative whites had overturned state and local fair housing laws in at least nine referenda, in some cases by arguing such antidiscrimination laws gave "special protections" to African-Americans. Now conservatives who were still hostile to civil rights appealed to black voters by warning that the extension of such laws to homosexuals would somehow mitigate the protections available to racial minorities, who they now said deserved "special protection" because of their historical experience of discrimination. At the same time, the charge that gays were demanding "special rights" also allowed Christian conservatives to play on the growing white hostility toward affirmative action.[20]

Conservatives' appeals to both groups were buttressed by their depiction of gays as a wealthy and politically powerful

elite that controlled the media and thus were especially unde-
serving of protection. But following Anita Bryant's lead, antigay activists also played to voters' fears by reviving other demonic stereotypes of homosexuals that allowed them to turn
the vote into a referendum on sexual practices instead of discrimination. Right-wing groups flooded states and cities with
antigay hate literature that depicted homosexuals as sex-crazed
perverts who threatened the nation's children and moral character. Repeated screenings in churches and on cable of two
antigay videos, "The Gay Agenda" and "Gay Rights, Special
Rights," mass mailings, and door-to-door and pew-to-pew
distribution of antigay pamphlets fostered a climate of hostility and fear during the referenda that was difficult for outsiders to fathom.

The growing right wing assault on gay rights and the ur-
gency of the AIDS crisis led to one of the most remarkable
and influential developments of the late 1980s: Unprecedented numbers of people came out to their heterosexual
friends, workmates, and families, and even more people followed their lead in the 1990s as the visibility and acceptance
of gay people palpably increased. Their commitment to edu-
cating and if necessary confronting the people closest to them
resulted in countless moments of struggle, debate, and soul
searching in families, workplaces, and elsewhere, which cu-
mulatively contributed mightily to the broad shifts in attitudes toward homosexuality. Relatively few lesbians and gay
men joined gay political organizations, but their efforts to
change the people around them transformed the gay movement into a mass movement. Their efforts collectively constituted a massive and remarkably successful grassroots cam-

paign to challenge the misconceptions and daily habits sustaining antigay bigotry.

Polling data suggest the magnitude of the shift. In 1985 only a quarter of Americans reported that a friend, relative, or co-worker had personally told them that they were gay, and more than half believed they did not know anyone gay. Fifteen years later, in 2000, the number of people who knew someone openly gay had tripled to three-quarters of the population, and only a fifth reported not knowing anyone gay.[21]

These were not just casual acquaintances. The number of Americans who reported having a gay friend or close acquaintance doubled from 1985 to 1994 (from 22 to 43 percent), and rose to 56 percent by 2000. Most remarkably, the percentage reporting that someone in their family was gay or lesbian jumped from 9 percent in 1992 to 23 percent in 2000. Whether that increase represents dramatic growth in the number of people coming out to their families or simply in people's willingness to tell a pollster about a gay relative, it speaks to the seismic cultural change that took place in the 1990s.[22] Another sign of that shift was provided by the explosive growth in the 1980s and 1990s of Parents and Friends of Lesbians and Gays, a group that started in the spring of 1973 when twenty parents of gay children met in a church in Greenwich Village to provide mutual support. By 1998, it had grown to be a national organization with nearly 500 chapters and 80,000 members. Along with giving parents a place to work through their feelings upon learning their children were gay, the organization became an important advocate of gay rights on the national stage.

As a result of both individual and collective efforts, gay political clout and cultural visibility grew in many parts of the country. A growing number of Democratic politicians from big cities or liberal college towns began showing up at gay pride marches as they realized that lesbians, gay men, and their supporters were an important constituency. Gay film festivals spread from San Francisco and New York to dozens of smaller cities, became month-long events, and showcased a growing body of work produced by independent queer filmmakers. Gay neighborhoods appeared across the country. Just as significantly, increasing numbers of lesbians and gay men felt comfortable being openly gay outside of those neighborhoods, at work, and at school. A growing number of heterosexuals took up the gay cause as their own.

For all their intensity, the heated discussions and bitter battles that took place at workplaces, dinner tables, and city council meetings over gay rights and AIDS policy largely remained below the national political horizon through most of the 1980s. But they set the stage for the explosive national debut of the gay movement in the 1990s, when first the military and then marriage captured the attention of Congress and the public alike.

Both the growing polarization of the nation over homosexuality and a distinct shift toward support for gay people were evident in the presidential election of 1992, when gay issues moved to the center of national debate for the first time. The gay movement seemed poised to take an enormous step forward with the election of the first president in the nation's history to speak decisively in support of gay rights, although the limits of that embrace were equally telling. Bill Clinton gained the enthusiastic backing of gay voters and donors despite the fact that he had no record whatsoever on gay issues in Arkansas and had even refused to meet with gay groups there. But at a major gay fundraising event for his campaign in Los Angeles, Clinton gave a powerful speech in which he promised that gay people were part of his "vision" for America and that he would end military discrimination "with the stroke of a pen." The polarization of the nation's electorate over gay rights meant few politicians with national aspirations were likely to say much more. But gay voters were so starved for recognition and support from a national candidate (and so desperate to back a winner after twelve years of right-wing influence in the White House) that it was enough to win him more than seven out of ten gay votes.[23]

Clinton won the presidency in part because the Republican incumbent, George H. W. Bush, let the Christian right take over his nominating convention in order to shore up their support. The harsh antigay and "traditional family values" rhetoric of Pat Robertson and Pat Buchanan, who declared that there was a "culture war" underway "for the soul of America," frightened many voters. Clinton's victory appeared to mark a decisive defeat for the New Right.

But the firestorm ignited by Clinton's proposal to end the military's ban on homosexuals quickly turned his postelection honeymoon into a political nightmare and revealed just how deeply polarized the nation remained. The public outcry against his plan had been stoked by years of right-wing organizing. The intransigence of the Pentagon brass and the outpouring of public opposition (calls to Congress ran a hundred to one against lifting the ban) were cultivated and orchestrated by the same conservative religious groups that had already undertaken dozens of local antigay campaigns; they saw the military debate as merely the latest battle in an ongoing cultural war against the threat homosexuality posed to the nation's survival as a Christian republic.

The volatile state of public attitudes could also be seen in the fate of the two statewide referendum initiatives settled in the November 1992 election. Voters in Oregon defeated Measure 9, which would have overturned existing local gay rights ordinances and required the government to teach that homosexuality is "wrong, unnatural, and perverse." That wording appeared to be too extreme for most voters. But on the same day, voters in Colorado passed Amendment 2, an amendment to the state constitution that lacked Oregon's sharp language but banned any municipality or unit of the government from enacting antigay discrimination ordinances or policies. This not only repealed the ordinances already enacted by Denver, Boulder, and Aspen, but effectively removed gay rights from the political agenda by preempting any future effort to secure antidiscrimination legislation. Conservative activists in nine states promptly announced their intention to seek similar constitutional amendments.[24]

The New World of the 1990s

Despite the gays-in-the-military debacle and others that would follow, the 1990s marked a major turning point in the place of lesbians and gay men in American society. The number of openly gay elected public officials jumped from 52 in 1991 to 146 by April 1998; there had been a total of only 50 in the entire period before 1990.[25] President Clinton never again let a gay issue dominate his administration's agenda, but he became the first president to appoint openly gay officials (more than 150) to his administration, to nominate an openly gay ambassador, the philanthropist and quiet activist James C. Hormel, or to invite gay leaders into the Oval Office. He also issued executive orders banning discrimination in the federal workplace on the basis of sexual orientation and barring the use of sexual orientation as a criterion for determining security clearance. The federal government, which once prohibited the employment of homosexuals, now prohibited its agencies from discriminating against them in employment.

Following the government's lead and under pressure from their own employees and unions, private employers followed suit. In 2002, a survey of 319 of America's largest companies found that approximately "92 percent of the firms surveyed prohibit workplace discrimination against gays and lesbians."[26]

In 1996, the Supreme Court ruled in *Romer v. Evans* that Colorado's Amendment 2 was unconstitutional. In sweeping language, it declared that no one could be made a stranger to the law and implicitly rejected the snide dismissal of gay rights in its *Bowers* decision a decade earlier. The number of antigay rights initiatives fell precipitously, although they continued to haunt the movement. Over the decade the number of municipalities and counties with gay rights ordinances lept from 80 in 1990 to more than 200 in 2000.[27]

At least as significant as these political developments was the dramatic growth in the visibility and acceptance of lesbians and gay men in the mass media in the nineties. Hollywood released a handful of films with significant gay characters or themes after the lifting of the censorship code in the 1960s, and network television, always a more timid medium in the era before cable, had introduced some gay characters in the 1970s. But it was only in the 1990s that lesbian and gay images, often positive and increasingly diverse and complex, permeated the mass media—from *Roseanne* to *Ellen*, from MTV to the nightly news, and from the *National Enquirer* to the *New York Times*.

Following the trail blazed by *Longtime Companion* and other independent films, *Philadelphia*, the first Hollywood studio film to address AIDS, was a huge success in 1993. Unlike earlier films, *Philadelphia* was a conventional melodrama that ignored the existence of the gay world or AIDS service organizations. But it featured some of Hollywood's biggest names, and its box office gross in the United States alone was fifteen times larger than that of *Longtime Companion*. *Philadelphia* starred Tom Hanks as a lawyer fired from his firm after being diagnosed with AIDS. The film followed Hanks's attorney (and nongay audience surrogate), Denzel Washington, as his growing friendship with Hanks led him to discard his misconceptions about gay men and people with AIDS. When Hanks received an Oscar for the role, millions saw him thank his openly gay high school drama coach. Three years later, a highly successful comedy, *The Birdcage*, sympathetically portrayed the devoted relationship between a gay father and club owner (Robin Williams) and his drag-queen partner (Nathan Lane), who had raised a son together. When Williams tried to hide his relationship and very openly gay life from the bigoted parents of their son's fiancée at the son's request, the film made the closet itself seem ridiculous as well as unjust. A small but growing number of celebrities from k.d. lang to Melissa Etheridge subsequently came out (or, like Rock Hudson, were forced out by AIDS-related illness), and other celebrities publicly embraced the gay cause.[28]

The growth in the number of gay characters on television was even more dramatic. In November 1989 ABC lost more than $1 million in advertising revenues when skittish sponsors withdrew from an episode of the immensely popular *thirtysomething* because it briefly showed two gay men in bed together. ABC decided not to include that episode in summer reruns, and the following year, only one show on any network had an ongoing gay character. But there were thirty-four regular lesbian, gay, bisexual, or transgender characters on television during the 1996–1997 season, which also witnessed Ellen Degeneres become the first title character of a series to come out—an act that seemed so momentous at the time that it generated months of speculation and landed Degeneres on the cover of *Time*. By the time *Will & Grace* premiered on NBC and quickly rose to the top of the charts two years later, gay and lesbian characters were a regular part of the television landscape.[29] It would be hard to overstate how much this changed the dominant representation of gay people. In the 1950s, homosexuals had almost always appeared in the press and occasional film as shadowy and ominous figures. But television and the movies suddenly turned them into a diverse and familiar group whose struggles and pleasures appealed to large viewing audiences. Gay people became part of the cultural landscape even for people without openly gay friends.

As people became more familiar with gay people, public support for gay rights grew. Only 56 percent of Americans supported gay rights legislation in 1977. This figure increased to 71 percent in 1989, and leapt to 84 percent seven years later, another sign of the dramatic shift that took place in the 1990s. Strikingly, by 2000 a significant majority of Americans still expressed moral disapproval of homosexuality, but a growing ethos of tolerance led many of the same people to oppose discrimination against homosexuals. A 2002 Gallup Poll found that even though 44 percent of the people said homosexuality was an unacceptable "alternative lifestyle," 86 percent thought homosexuals should have "equal rights in terms of job opportunities." The contrast was even more striking among African-Americans, who were more supportive of gay civil rights than whites even though they also expressed more moral disapproval of homosexuality.[30]

Yet regional differences in the support of gay rights remained. Polls showed that public opinion in Massachusetts, Connecticut, and Hawaii was the most progay. Progay sentiment was also strong in most other states in New England, in New Jersey and New York, and in other regional clusters: Maryland in the mid-Atlantic, Wisconsin, Minnesota, and Illinois in the upper Midwest, California, Oregon, and Washington on the West Coast. Antigay sentiment was strongest in Mississippi and other southern states, as well as in the lower Midwest and plains states. Even in hostile regions, however, gay people could find outposts of tolerance in college towns or large cities such as Austin, Houston, or Atlanta. But the striking regional polarization of the nation could be seen not just in public opinion polls but also in regional variations in congressional votes on key gay issues, in the outcomes of lesbian custody cases, and in the passage of gay rights laws. Only two states—Wisconsin in 1982 and Massachusetts in 1989—enacted legislation banning antigay discrimination before 1990. The number rose to eleven by 2000, but eight of the states were in the Northeast or on the Pacific Coast.[31]

By the mid-1990s, then, lesbians and gay men faced a complex mixture of support and hostility. There were still no laws protecting them from discrimination in jobs or public accommodations in four-fifths of the fifty states, a fact that had palpable consequences for people's lives and livelihoods. Long before the murder of Wyoming college student Matthew Shepherd in 1998 brought national attention to the problem, adults remained acutely aware that no matter how comfortable or accepted they felt in some neighborhoods, simply holding a partner's hand could provoke a violent response. The continuing threat of antigay vigilante violence, particularly in a culture in which open expressions of heterosexual affection evoked smiles, was a constant reminder of persistent hostility. Transgender people of color faced even more violence, which continued to receive less attention.

Nevertheless, when Matthew Shepherd's murder provoked a national outcry and even the president spoke out against antigay violence, it was clear that a profound change had taken place. After years of prosecutors and judges dismissing attacks on gay people as predictable rites of youth, the gay anti-violence movement had succeeded in making the authorities—and the public—recognize such violence as a serious problem.

The results of half a century of struggle were everywhere evident. In the 1990s, there were annual gay pride marches in more than 100 cities. There were influential gay caucuses in the major unions and strong movements seeking reform in the Catholic Church and every mainline Protestant denomination. Gay choruses sprung up in small towns, and the gay square dancing movement took off nationally. An edgy "new queer cinema" and increasing numbers of Hollywood films featured gay characters. For three years running (1992–94), plays by the openly gay playwrights Tony Kushner and Terrence McNally won the Tony for Best Play. In June 1994, a million people gathered in New York to celebrate the 25th anniversary of the Stonewall rebellion. They took over Yankee Stadium for a celebratory concert and thronged the Gay Games, a quadrinneal gay sporting event modelled on the Olympics that drew lesbian and gay athletes from around the world.

The movement's success had a palpable impact on people's lives. Many lesbians and gay men participated in a rich and supportive gay life. Equally important, many no longer found it necessary to hide their gayness or their partners in order to participate in the larger social life of their communities. They took their partners home for the holidays, debated the merits of the latest gay film with their heterosexual colleagues, and increasingly assumed they would be accepted on their own terms. A growing number of couples held commitment ceremonies attended by their parents and siblings along with gay and straight friends alike. Many gay youth, and even many heterosexuals, found it hard to believe it had ever been different. The fact that gay couples did not receive the same recognition, protections, or rights that heterosexual couples took for granted began to seem anomalous, not just to many gay people but to their married brothers and sisters.

Marriage rights for gay couples would not have become imaginable without the place of gay people in American society having changed so much. Even so, they were barely on the agenda for gay people, let alone the nation, in the 1980s and early 1990s.

Why did marriage emerge as such an urgent issue for so many gay people that it could galvanize thousands to line up outside San Francisco's city hall? And why did it emerge as such an explosive issue for the nation? To answer this, we need first to understand how marriage itself had changed.

THREE

How Marriage Changed

$\mathcal{M}$ ARRIAGE IS CONSTANTLY CHANGING. Once often polygamous, it is now usually monogamous. Once concerned primarily with the control of labor and the transmission of property, now it is supposed to nurture happiness and mutual commitment. Once governed by custom alone, it has been alternately regulated by kin, slaveowners, masters, church, and state. Given the enormous variation over time and among cultures in how "marriage" has organized sexual and emotional life, child-rearing, property, kinship, and political alliances, many anthropologists are loathe to use the term "marriage" at all, since the term's apparently straightforward simplicity hides so much more than it reveals.[1]

Four fundamental changes in marriage since the nineteenth century have made the right to marry seem both more imaginable and more urgent to lesbians and gay men. In its own time each of these changes seemed as momentous as the prospect of same-sex marriage does today. First, the right to choose one's partner in marriage, no matter how much that choice distressed one's family, ethnic community, and co-religionists, came to be seen as a fundamental civil right. Second, the sharp differences in the marital roles assigned husbands and wives declined, so that it became easier to imagine a marriage between two people of the same gender. Third, marriage became a crucial nexus for the allocation of public and private rights and benefits, so that the exclusion of same-sex couples from marriage imposed increasingly significant economic and legal consequences. Finally, the power of any one religious group to impose its marriage rules on others, while never strong, sharply declined. Most of these changes were once opposed on the grounds that they violated God's will, threatened the established social order, and thwarted the purposes of nature. Each of them has now been embraced by most Americans as a moral good and the "commonsense" way marriage should be.

The most passionate opponents of same-sex marriage today are often the same people most reluctant to embrace these other changes. If its advocates regard same-sex marriage as a logical next step in marriage's evolution toward freedom and equality, its most vociferous opponents see it as one more sign of marriage's degeneration.

The Freedom to Choose One's Marital Partner Became a Fundamental Civil Right

The most important change is that the freedom to marry, and above all the freedom to choose one's partner in marriage, has come to be seen by the courts and the American people as a fundamental civil right. This was not always the case, since parents sometimes interfered with their children's decisions and numerous laws once sought to prevent "immoral" or "unnatural" couplings, especially across the color line. But the origins of the belief that the freedom to marry is a civil right can nonetheless be seen in the colonial American conception of marriage. Drawing on Christian precepts, the colonists saw consent on the part of both man and woman as a fundamental condition of marriage. For generations, in fact, the couple's mutual consent to the marital relationship was considered more important than official recognition by the state or church, and that recognition usually followed from the couple's own declaration of their status.[2]

As the importance of contract ideology grew in the Revolutionary era, marriage was most commonly described as a contract whose legitimacy rested on the mutual consent of both parties. So important was consent to the legitimation of marriage that the consensual ties of husband and wife became a compelling metaphor for the relations of citizens to their new government. The people must consent to their government, as to their marriage—though more conservative writers added that once the citizenry had consented to the leadership of an official, they were obliged to follow it, as a wife must follow her husband after consenting to marry him.[3] Carrying through with the metaphor, most states established a limited right of divorce for specified grounds (usually adultery), since the Revolutionary model required that people be allowed to withdraw their consent when the marital contract, no less than the governmental contract, had been broken. As the historian Nancy Cott put it, "How could consent in marriage (as in government) be considered fully voluntary, if it could not be withdrawn by an injured party?"[4]

The conviction that the freedom to marry was a fundamental civil right became more emphatic in the nineteenth century during the great national debate over slavery. Slaves had no right to marry, since they had no standing to make contracts of any kind and because obligations to a spouse might interfere with their obligations to their master. Many slaves nonetheless established informal marriages that were honored among other slaves and often even recognized by their masters. But slaveowners did not feel obliged—nor were they obliged by law or custom—to let such marriages interfere with their use of slaves, even if it meant separating a couple by sale. Abolitionists decried slavery's degradation of the marital relationship as one of its greatest moral failings. After the Civil War, newly freed men and women wandered the region in search of partners lost to sale. Having felt the harsh power of their masters, they crowded the offices of the Freedmen's Bureau to insist on the legal recognition and protection of their marital oaths. The freedom to marry and secure their families was one of the most palpable freedoms claimed by former slaves, one of the most personally consequential signs that they were now free citizens, not subject to another's whim. As one Virginia member of the Colored Infantry declared, "The Marriage Covenant is at the foundation of all our rights."[5]

But in much of the country, the former slaves' new freedom to marry only increased white concerns about whom they would marry. Statutes banning interracial marriage dated from early in the colonial period—Maryland enacted the first such ban in the 1660s—but "it was not until after the demise of slavery that they began to function as the ultimate sanction of the American system of white supremacy," as historian

Peggy Pascoe shows. During the Civil War and Reconstruction, a flurry of states enacted laws banning interracial marriage or even interracial sex (often called miscegenation, a new word the Democratic opponents of "race-mixing" invented to discredit Lincoln's Republican Party in the 1864 campaign). The black codes passed by Southern states after the war to limit the freedom of former slaves all included prohibitions against such marriages.

Similar bans already existed across the nation, but as fears about racial mixing grew in the late nineteenth and early twentieth century, a flurry of new Northern and Western states passed such laws as well. Fourteen states, primarily in the West, extended the ban to include marriages between whites and Asians, and twelve states to white marriages with American Indians. Forty-one states or territories had enacted such bans by 1913, when Wyoming became the last state to do so. A last flurry of legislative activity followed the national uproar caused when Jack Johnson, the first black professional heavyweight boxing champion, married a white woman and then was prosecuted and convicted under the Mann (or White Slavery) Act of 1910 for inducing a white woman to cross state lines for purposes of prostitution. A congressman from Georgia proposed a constitutional amendment prohibiting marriage between "persons of color and Caucasians," in order, he said on the floor of the House, "to uproot and exterminate now this debasing, ultrademoralizing, un-American, and inhuman leprosy." Even two of the few remaining states without interracial marriage bans, Vermont in 1912 and Massachusetts in 1913, passed laws forbidding couples whose marriages would be prohibited in their home states from traveling there to get married. [6]

States passed such laws because Emancipation, the postwar civil rights acts, black migration to the North and West, and Chinese immigration to the West all made lawmakers realize that the common prejudice against interracial marriages— and the common-sense assumption that they were unthinkable—could no longer be relied on to prevent them. The problem was particularly acute in the South, where black freedom and political mobilization posed unprecedented challenges to white domination. Southern white officials stepped up their policing of sex as well as marriage between black men and white women, making its prohibition a powerful sign of the limits of black equality

The tide began to turn against race-based marriage bans in the mid-twentieth century, when the Nazi laws forbidding Jews from marrying non-Jews discredited such bans along with many other expressions of state racism. In 1948 the General Assembly of the United Nations unanimously adopted the Universal Declaration of Human Rights, which proclaimed that the "right to marry" was one of the fundamental rights of humankind.[7] That same year, the California Supreme Court became the first high state court to buck the tide of public opinion by holding that the state's ban on interracial marriage was inconsistent with the constitutional guarantee of equality. "The essence of the right to marry," it declared in *Perez v. Sharp*, "is freedom to join in marriage with the person of one's choice."[8] Nineteen years later, the Supreme Court made such freedom the law of the land when it declared in *Loving v. Virginia* that

The freedom to marry has long been recognized as one of the vital personal rights essential to the orderly pursuit of happiness by free men. Marriage is one of the "basic civil rights of man," fundamental to our very existence and survival. . . . Under our Constitution, the freedom to marry, or not marry, a person of another race resides with the individual and cannot be infringed by the State.[9]

In a sweeping statement in its historic 1967 decision, the court recognized that the ban on interracial marriage was "designed to maintain White Supremacy" and thus could not withstand the constitutional requirements of equality. To fully recognize the civil rights of people of color meant recognizing their right to choose their partner in marriage. In the coming years, the Court continued to extend the reach of that freedom, deciding, for instance, that even prisoners could not be denied their civil right to marry.[10]

In 2003, the Massachusetts Supreme Judicial Court built on those precedents when it extended this right to lesbians and gay men. "In this case, as in *Perez* and *Loving*," the court declared, "a statute deprives individuals of access to an institution of fundamental legal, personal, and social significance—the institution of marriage—because of a single trait: skin color in *Perez* and *Loving*, sexual orientation here. As it did in *Perez* and *Loving*, history must yield to a more fully developed understanding of the invidious quality of the discrimination."[11]

This shift in attitude was not limited to the courts. Most Americans came to accept the right of their children, relatives, friends, and co-religionists to choose their partner in marriage, even if they found the choice distasteful or distressing. Almost three-quarters of white Americans (and nine out of ten white Southerners) still disapproved of interracial marriages when *Loving* was decided, and almost half supported laws banning them. It wasn't until thirty-four years later, in 1991, that a plurality of white Americans told a pollster they approved of them. But the great majority came to accept them, however begrudgingly.[12] Attitudes toward interfaith marriage are equally telling. Even today, many parents of deep faith are disappointed when their children choose to marry someone of a different faith. But they accept that it is their children's own choice to make. The new consensus in support of marital choice has contributed to the belief of many lesbians and gay men that it is their right to marry the partner of their choice as well. It may also ultimately lead more Americans to accept their right to do so, even if they abhor the idea of same-sex marriage as much as their parents and grandparents abhorred interracial or interfaith marriage.

Marriage Became More Gender-Neutral and Egalitarian

Marriage also became more inviting—indeed, more imaginable—for same-sex couples as the sharp differences in the roles assigned by gender to husband and wife declined. Historically, marriage was one of the primary social institutions through which gender difference and inequality were produced. As the historian Nancy Cott puts it, "Turning men and women into husbands and wives, marriage has designated the ways both sexes act in the world and the reciprocal relation between them. It has done so probably more emphatically than any other single institution or social force."[13]

Two hundred years ago, when a woman consented to a marriage, it was the last time she could consent to a legal agreement on her own. When she took her husband's name, her legal identity was absorbed into his and she lost most of her rights as a citizen. Well into the nineteenth century, under the system known as coverture, she lost the capacity to enter into contracts or sue in court. Her personal property and earnings became the property of her husband, to whom she owed her labor, companionship, and obedience. In return, he had to provide for her and take responsibility for her premarital debts. She was defined by her dependence on him, and he by the independence and social stature he gained as the head of a household. As the historian John Demos observes, the household was "a little commonwealth," headed and represented in the larger community by the husband and father. The marriage ceremony pronounced the couple "man and wife" because the man's legal status changed so little compared to the woman's.[14]

However feasible in an agrarian economy, this marriage regime could not survive the growth of the wage economy and its ideology of free labor. Feminist marriage reformers drew analogies to slavery to describe women's position in marriage: their lack of self-possession and inability to engage in contracts on their own authority. In the mid-nineteenth century, most states enacted Married Women's Property Acts that gave women the right to own property, to sue and be sued, and to enter into contracts. But the assumption that wives were wards of their husbands continued to influence the courts, legislatures, and public opinion. One reason that marriage became such a fundamental sign of full citizenship and manhood to men freed from slavery was that it allowed them to establish households in which they governed their wives and children and had command of their labor. In the political ideology of post–Civil War Reconstruction, the subordination of women to men through the marriage contract was central to the very definition of men's freedom.[15]

The enduring power of the conviction that women lost their autonomy when they married was made clear in the arguments made against granting women the vote in the early twentieth century. Women's suffrage, its opponents charged, would irrevocably undermine the family as it had been known for millennia. The marital bond would be threatened with untold divisions, they warned, if wives could cast ballots that countermanded those of their husbands, if they had reason to follow political debate and might end up disagreeing with their husbands. Social stability itself, these traditionalists insisted, depended on well-ordered families united in purpose. Like those who would oppose gay rights three generations later, they often found justification for their opposition to women's suffrage in Genesis and St. Paul. Former president Grover Cleveland, for one, pointed to "the division of Divine purpose clearly shown when Adam was put in the Garden of Eden to dress it and keep it, and Eve was given to him as a helpmeet and because it was not good that man should be alone."[16]

Women—even wives—gained the vote in 1920 with passage of the Nineteenth Amendment, but marriage continued to impose legal and economic disabilities on women well into the twentieth century. The 1907 immigration act decreed that a woman automatically lost her United States citizenship if she married a foreigner, and wives' independent claim to citizenship was only fully recognized in the 1930s. During the Great Depression, many states passed laws requiring that women employed by the government be fired if they got married, on the theory that their husbands could take care of them and other men would need the jobs. Employers justified paying women lower wages for equal work because they were supposedly just earning "pin money" for frivolous purchases, their real support coming from their fathers or husbands. In the 1950s, married women with good jobs still found it difficult to get loans or credit cards without their husband's signature.[17]

Although gender roles and inequality have hardly disappeared from marriage, there has been something of a revolution in marriage law and the lived experience of marriage since the 1970s, due in substantial part to the feminist lawsuits that resulted in requirements that laws, including laws pertaining to the family, treat men and women the same. Most of the legal rights and obligations of marriage, which once were strictly distinguished by gender, have become gender-neutral and mutual. Before the 1970s, only husbands were required to support their wives, but since then that has been a mutual obligation. In the 1970s, wives gained the right to sue third parties who injured their husbands, when the injury resulted in loss of their husband's companionship and support. Before then, only husbands could sue for such losses, because under common law only they were owed such companionship and support. Court-ordered divorce settlements were also transformed in the 1970s and 1980s. Sometimes by custom, often by law, courts had long crafted arrangements based on set assumptions about the distinctive capacities of all men and all women rather than on the particular circumstances of the parties involved. The new divorce regime made it easier for couples to divorce and made fewer assumptions about who would have a better job or be a better parent. It tailored arrangements for alimony, child custody and support, and the division of marital property to the couple's actual circumstances. Husbands and wives now owed one another the same things and could claim the same rights. At least in law, marriage became a relationship between equals.[18]

Marriage continued to confer on people a special status that granted them collective rights in relation to outsiders and imposed on them special obligations to one another. But as a legal matter those obligations lost their gender specificity, and couples became freer to negotiate their own arrangements. Women are still more likely to stay at home with the children, do more housework, and earn less when they work outside the home. But such inequalities are no longer structured by law.[19]

As a result, growing numbers of heterosexual couples have come to resemble gay couples in the sense that their roles in their relationship are no longer determined by gender. To put it another way, there continues to be a division of labor in marriage: who wakes up with the kids and who puts them to bed, who fixes dinner and who washes the dishes. But distinct family roles are no longer arbitrarily assigned to the "husband" or the "wife." Even though many wives continue to bear a disproportionate share of such tasks, many husbands today are more involved in child-rearing, grocery shopping, and housekeeping than their fathers were. This change makes the idea that marriage can only consist of a man and woman no longer appear as obvious or necessary to many people as it once did.

Marriage Became a Primary Nexus for the Allocation of State and Private Benefits

The vision of a male-headed and -dominated household may no longer structure the law of marriage itself, but it continues to structure many of the social insurance or welfare programs put in place over the course of the twentieth century. Marriage acquired a unique status in the United States as the nexus for the allocation of a host of public and private benefits. While every other industrialized society made health care and old-age security a right of citizenship, the tenuous "security net" created in the United States in the twentieth century made access to many benefits contingent on employment or marriage. As a result, if marriage became thinkable for lesbians and gay men because of the ways in which it changed, access to the rights and benefits marriage provided also came to seem more urgent as those rights and benefits multiplied. This was a distinctly American approach, and one consequence has been that the stakes in the marriage debate in the United States have been especially high.[20]

Beginning with veteran's pensions and mother's pensions in the late nineteenth and early twentieth centuries, the United

States constructed a social insurance system that was less secure and generous than those developed by the other industrialized democracies, primarily in Europe, whose comprehensive social insurance programs were available to all. The United States created a mixed public–private insurance system linked to employment and premised on the assumption that most Americans would be part of a male-headed household consisting of a male breadwinner and female homemaker, and serving, in many cases, to make divergence from that norm costly. The Economic Security Act of 1935 was the landmark legislation establishing old-age insurance (what we now call social security) and unemployment insurance as entitlements for people who participated in the labor market, as well as a second-tier, means-tested system of aid to the disabled, women with dependent children, and others who did not have jobs. As the General Accounting Office (GAO) reported to Congress in 1996, "recognition of the marital relationship is integral to the design of the program. . . . Once the law sets forth the basic right of an individual participant to retirement benefits, it prescribes in great detail the corresponding rights of the current or former spouse. Whether one is eligible for Social Security payments, and if so how much one receives, are both dependent on marital status."[21]

The expansion of the American welfare state has only multiplied the ways that the marital relationship shapes the allocation of government benefits. After the Civil War, the government provided pensions to veterans of the Grand Army of the Republic who had saved the Union, but it dramatically expanded such benefits during the Second World War with the GI Bill of Rights. An astonishing piece of social engineering, the GI Bill financed much of the postwar suburban building boom, paid for the higher education or job training of returning veterans (and covered their expenses while in school), served as an affirmative action program for postwar men by giving veterans preferential access to many jobs, and effectively channeled people into the male-headed, suburban, single-family homes usually described as the "natural" or "traditional" family pattern of the 1950s. The government continues to provide a vast array of benefits to veterans and their spouses—but only to spouses who can marry them. According to the GAO, "A surviving spouse . . . of a veteran is entitled to receive monthly dependency and indemnity compensation payments when the veteran's death was service-connected, and to receive a monthly pension when the veteran's death was not service-connected," and may be entitled to "educational assistance for up to 45 months, job counseling, training, and placement services." But only if they were married.[22]

The federal income tax, authorized by a constitutional amendment in 1913, became a mass tax only when the government struggled to pay the staggering costs of the Second World War (while only 7 million people were taxed in 1940, 45 million were taxed by war's end). Although originally all taxpayers were taxed as individuals, the wartime expansion of the tax base precipitated a debate about how married couples should be treated. New legislation in 1948 introduced the "joint return" for married couples. Once again based on the presumption that "normal families" consisted of an employed husband and a dependent wife who stayed at home, the new policy allowed such couples to pool their income for tax purposes, which had the effect of significantly lowering a married man's tax burden. As dual-income families became more common, the pooling of income ironically increased the tax burden on married couples (with similar incomes) by raising their tax bracket. In this one respect, unmarried same-sex couples gained an advantage over their married counterparts.[23]

But most of the new tax regime imposed severe disadvantages on unmarried same-sex couples. As the GAO reported, "the distinction between married and unmarried status is pervasive in federal tax law." The effects could be especially catastrophic for elderly couples who had bought homes together, or who sought to transfer assets between one another, or who faced staggering taxes when a widowed partner discovered the IRS did not recognize their joint ownership of property for inheritance tax purposes. According to the GAO, "For estate tax purposes, property transferred to one spouse as the result of the death of another is deductible for purposes of determining the value of the decedent's estate. . . . These provisions permit married couples to transfer substantial sums to one another, and to third parties, without tax liability in circumstances in which single people would not enjoy the same privilege." And same-sex couples, even if they shared resources for decades, were considered "single people," or legal strangers, by the IRS.

One of the peculiarities of the American social insurance system is that Americans depend on their employers, instead of the state, for many crucial benefits. The family became the nexus for the allocation of private benefits as well. No company offered its employees pensions before the late nineteenth century. The dramatic expansion in private pension programs took place during the Second World War, when they became a way for companies to compete for workers while wages were frozen, and in the immediate postwar years, when companies saw them as a useful way to solidify worker loyalty and unions saw them as a crucial hedge against the inadequate retirement income provided by the government. In the years following the Second World War, when most Western European democracies were establishing programs that entitled every citizen and resident to health care, large corporations and medical associations persuaded the U.S. Congress to reject President Truman's proposals for national health insurance, and those same private employers began to offer health insurance programs themselves. By 1965, most people depended on their employer—or their spouse's employer—for their health insurance, life insurance, and the better part of their retirement income—if they had these benefits at all. By 1990, such benefits came to account for about 30 percent of an employee's overall compensation.[24]

Federal legislation designed to regulate private insurance programs often served to compound the disadvantage faced by same-sex couples who could not get married. For instance, the Employee Retirement Income Security Act of 1974, known as ERISA, required company retirement and annuity plans to protect the interests of spouses, but not of unmarried partners. The Consolidated Omnibus Budget Reconciliation Act of 1986, known as COBRA, required companies to allow employees who had lost their job—and their spouses—to continue to purchase health coverage for up to 18 months, and to allow the surviving spouse of a deceased employee to purchase such coverage. But unmarried partners were (and still are) not afforded access to such coverage. In a similar manner, the Family and Medical Leave Act of 1994 makes it possible for employees to take an unpaid leave from work for up to twelve weeks a year (without risking their jobs) to take care of a spouse, parent, or child with health problems—but not to take care of a dying unmarried partner.[25]

Inequities were also built into the programs developed by the government to supplement the programs offered by large employers. Consider two health insurance programs established by Congress in 1965 to fill in the holes left by private programs. The more generous program, Medicare, made health care an entitlement for people who had worked before they turned 65 and then lost their company insurance upon retirement. Medicaid provided less adequate needs-based health care to the unemployed and the working poor. Medicaid requires people to be virtually destitute or to spend down their resources before it will pay for medical care or nursing homes. But at least it protects the family home when a spouse must enter a nursing home. A home jointly owned by same-sex partners, by contrast, has to be sold to pay for nursing care before Medicaid kicks in, leaving the other partner homeless. Under current law, the healthy partner also needs to pay for legal documents guaranteeing the right to visit his or her partner in the nursing home or hospital, the right to make medical decisions for the partner if he or she is incapacitated, and the right to bury or otherwise take care of the partner's remains—all things a married couple could take for granted.[26]

The American social insurance system is rife with such financial and legal inequities, largely in part because it makes so many benefits, from health insurance to an adequate retirement income, dependent on a person (or a person's spouse) being employed by a company that provides them. Making the marital relationship the central nexus for the allocation of both public and private benefits has only compounded the inequities. The exclusion of same-sex couples—who cannot gain the legal status, rights, and benefits of marriage—from those benefits has threatened those couples with impoverishment and insecurity. As the Stonewall generation of lesbians and gay men began to age, they began to notice.

The Power of Religious Authorities to Impose Their Marriage Rules on Others Declined

Some opponents of same-sex marriage argue that marriage was originally a religious matter, a sacrament of the church, and thus should be left to the churches to govern. Grant same-sex couples "civil unions," the most liberal of them say, but preserve the religious view of marriage as exclusively the union of one man and one woman.

From the perspective of history, this argument quickly encounters two objections. The first is that it misconstrues and homogenizes the complex history of religious beliefs about marriage. Historically, the churches themselves have not agreed on the sacramental character of marriage, and in the last generation a growing number of faiths have begun to celebrate the marriages of same-sex couples. On the day same-sex marriage became legal in Massachusetts, the Unitarian Universalist Association, Reform Judaism, Reconstructionist

Judaism, and the Metropolitan Community Church encouraged their clergy to officiate at such weddings, and clergy in the American Baptist Churches and United Church of Christ could choose to do so. While the Roman Catholic Church, Episcopal Church, United Methodist Church, Presbyterian Church, National Baptist Convention, and several other Protestant and Orthodox denominations forbade their clergy to officiate at such weddings, this policy provoked passionate debate and faith-based opposition among the clergy in most of the Protestant denominations.[27]

By the spring of 2004, there was, in short, no single religious view on the matter. The proposed constitutional amendment restricting marriage to a man and a woman would give state sanction to one religious view of marriage while contravening other religious practices and beliefs.

But in addition to this, the religious argument against same-sex marriage ignores a fundamental historical fact about marriage in the United States: It has always been a civil matter. And the tolerance of the courts and the public for attempts by religious authorities to impose their marriage rules on others has declined sharply in the last half century.

In the beginning, marriage was an informal affair, governed by custom rather than by the church or state. A brief historical tour of marriage could reasonably start with Rome, whose legal code influenced every subsequent European legal system. In the days before Christianization, Romans considered men and women to be married once they began to share their lives and told others they regarded one another as husband and wife. They could end their marriages by separation, or desertion. As a practical matter, this custom endured for centuries (and still, in effect, governs most gay relationships and many nonmarital heterosexual couplings). Even though early Christian leaders began to believe that it should not be so easy to end marriages, that, indeed, a marriage should be indissoluble, the new Christian emperors did little to change the customary approach to marriage, since few people saw marriage as either a legal or canon matter. The Church sought to expand its authority over marriage after the collapse of the Roman Empire, but as one prominent scholar notes, "The greatest obstacle to the direct enforcement by the Church of the new Christian ideas about sex and marriage was that marriage was regarded everywhere in Europe in the first half of the Middle Ages as a personal and purely secular matter."[28] By the tenth century, ecclesiastical authorities had begun to establish their authority over proceedings that until then had been seen as purely personal in nature. But it was centuries before they fully succeeded. Christian leaders themselves long debated the character of marriage. A consensus about its sacramental character developed in the Roman Catholic Church only around the thirteenth century, and it was not adopted as a dogmatic truth until the Council of Florence in the mid-fifteenth century. It was only in the sixteenth century that the Catholic Church required a public ceremony and the presence of a priest for a marriage to be deemed valid. It did this largely to ensure parental consent to marriages that until then, at least in theory, had required only the agreement of the two consenting parties.

Control over marriage was one of the chief prizes in the long struggle between secular and religious authorities for power over everyday life. In Europe, the Roman Catholic

Church lost much of its new legal authority over marriage in the wake of the Reformation and Enlightenment, and the insistence of Martin Luther, among other Protestant reformers, that marriage was not a sacrament but a civil contract.

In Britain, the Church of England was able to maintain its authority over marriages somewhat longer. But the religious dissenters who colonized New England decisively rejected ecclesiastical regulation of marriage. They declared from the beginning that marriage was a civil contract. In the Anglican southern colonies, the Church of England nominally maintained its authority over marriage but never supplied enough clergy to make their regulation of marriages a practical possibility. After the American Revolution, all states recognized marriage as a purely civil matter. American citizens of various faiths might choose to have their marriages performed by clergy and might subject themselves to their churches' marriage rules, but this was purely voluntary on their part. As a legal matter, clergy officiated at marriages only as agents of the state, and marriages had legal standing only as a civil contract and status.[29]

The clearest sign of the civil character of marriage in the United States—and the one most relevant to the current debate—is this: The rules established by many churches restricting who may marry whom in a religious ceremony have not, in fact, been able to prevent people from getting married. The Roman Catholic Code of Canon Law promulgated in 1918 declared that "The Church most strictly and everywhere forbids marriages between a Catholic and a person enrolled in an heretical or schismatical sect [that is, a Protestant]."[30] In practice the ban was not quite so strict, since a dispensation was usually given if the non-Catholic party promised to raise the children in the Catholic faith. But without this pledge, Catholic clergy refused to officiate at the marriage of a Catholic to a non-Catholic, and until 1966 a Catholic who married before a non-Catholic minister faced excommunication.[31] Most Protestant denominations were no more sympathetic to such marriages, even if they did not forbid them. The Lutheran Church, Missouri Synod, for one, warned its members that mixed marriages "condemn unborn children to the soul-destroying religion of the antichrist." Other Protestant denominations, including the Presbyterians, Methodists, American Baptists, and Southern Baptists, issued statements in the 1940s and 1950s warning their members against marrying Roman Catholics.[32]

Religious warnings and even the threat of excommunication could not prevent marriages between Catholics and Protestants, however, since marriage was a state matter, not subject to such religious restrictions. Nor did the state enforce the prenuptial agreements signed by non-Catholics promising that the children would be raised as Catholics. From the 1910s through the 1950s, numerous court cases resulted when interfaith marriages ended in divorce, the non-Catholic parent (usually the mother) retained custody of the children and chose to raise them in her own faith, and the Catholic parent (usually the father) sued to enforce their prenuptial agreement. The courts almost uniformly refused to enforce church rules by making such agreements binding. The religious rules of marriage simply were not binding on the marital partners.[33]

Although the "rules" governing interfaith marriage rarely surfaced in the public debate over same-sex marriage in

Massachusetts, the memory of them influenced that debate in surprising ways. Standing in line to get her marriage license at Cambridge City Hall, Marcia Hams talked about a meeting she'd had with her state legislator, trying to persuade him not to support the proposed state constitutional amendment banning same-sex marriage. She knew he was under a lot of pressure from the church. So she told him a story about her partner's mother: "My partner's mother is Catholic. She married a non-Catholic. And if it were up to the Catholic Church, she could never have gotten married. The church wouldn't marry them. It had to be a civil marriage." That's what we're talking about here, she told him. "If the church controlled marriage completely, then there'd be a lot of people that couldn't get married. And he told me an incredible story in response to that. He told us that he had some friends who were engaged. And then the man had a car accident and became a paraplegic, so he couldn't reproduce. So the local priest in the church wouldn't marry them. So another priest had to do it." Marcia was still a bit stunned by the story. "We thought we were giving him an example" of why the church shouldn't control civil marriage, "and he gave us one that was even worse."

The influence of Protestant teaching on early American marriage law, especially its stress on the importance of consent, monogamy, and permanence, was important. But over the last two centuries, marriage has been influenced as much by the Revolutionary commitment to equality, the growing application of contract theory, and profound changes in the social, legal, and economic relations of men and women. The United States, once overwhelmingly Protestant, has become a society of many faiths. In 2000, only half of Americans identified themselves as Protestants, a quarter as Catholics, about a tenth as irreligious, and much smaller but significant numbers as Jews and Muslims, along with small but rapidly growing numbers as Hindus, Buddhists, and other faiths. As a result, the influence of any one particular religious tradition has declined.

Although various Protestant and Catholic groups have continued to try to impose their religion's marriage rules on others, they have found it increasingly difficult to do so. As in most marriage matters, the change has been especially striking in the last half century. Shifts in public opinion and new laws governing divorce and access to birth control provide the most powerful evidence of their declining influence.

After the Revolution, few American states banned divorce altogether, as some Catholic European countries did. But the Christian view that marriage should be a permanent bond influenced the law of divorce everywhere. Most states allowed people to end their marriages only if one spouse could prove that the other had violated certain specified rules of marriage. As a result, many couples that had agreed to terminate their marriages had to lie to the courts by admitting violations they had not committed, and in some states even staging them.

Some states reformed their laws to make them more congruent with reality, but the Catholic Church's opposition kept New York laws especially strict. In the 1930s, adultery was still the only acceptable grounds for divorce there. Women deserted by their husbands were unable to secure a divorce, and many people separated from spouses found themselves unable to remarry because they were unable to legally end their first marriage. In 1934, when a state legislator from the Upper West Side of New York proposed legislation making desertion a grounds for divorce, the Catholic Welfare Committee led the opposition. Its Secretary sent a memo to each assemblyman warning that "To weaken the law concerning the marital status is to strike at the foundation of society. The stability of the State itself is involved. Marriage is the basis of the family—and the family is the cornerstone of society." Despite an outpouring of letters in support of the measure, many from Catholic women deserted by their husbands, the legislation was soundly defeated. When the legislature considered divorce reform again fourteen years later, the movement faltered after the presiding judge of the Archdiocesan Tribunal of New York called the proposals "a menace to society."

Across the country, the divorce rate climbed slowly but surely. By the 1960s, 90 percent of divorces were uncontested, and the courts processed them on what one historian calls "an assembly-line basis," knowing full well that the grounds offered for divorce, adultery or some other infraction, were not true. In 1969, the California legislature voted to end the charade by making "irreconcilable differences" sufficient grounds for divorce. The character and severity of those differences was up to the couple, not the state, to determine, and neither party had to prove the other at fault. Unlike the marriage of gay couples, divorce reform affected everyone's marriage by introducing a new degree of freedom—and insecurity—to them. So-called "no-fault" divorce swept the country in the next fifteen years.[34]

Likewise, beginning in the late nineteenth century, the lobbying of religious groups (originally Protestant, later Catholic) led legislators to pass laws making it a crime in most of the nation to sell birth-control devices—even to married couples.[35] But in 1965 the Supreme Court ruled in *Griswold v. Connecticut* that such bans were an unconstitutional invasion of the privacy of the marital relationship. Seven years later it ruled in *Eisenstadt v. Baird* that even unmarried couples had the right to make such decisions about the conduct of their intimate lives. In 2003 the Supreme Court decisively extended that right to same-sex couples in *Lawrence v. Texas*. The Massachusetts Supreme Judicial Court based its decision to allow same-sex marriages in part on such considerations. As the Court explained:

> Many people hold deep-seated religious, moral, and ethical convictions that marriage should be limited to the union of one man and one woman, and that homosexual conduct is immoral. Many hold equally strong religious, moral, and ethical convictions that same-sex couples are entitled to be married, and that homosexual persons should be treated no differently than their heterosexual neighbors. Neither view answers the question before us. Our concern is with the Massachusetts Constitution as a charter of governance for every person properly within its reach. [Quoting the *Lawrence* decision, it added,] "Our obligation is to define the liberty of all, not to mandate our own moral code."[36]

One way of viewing the privacy doctrine established by *Griswold*—the constitutional principle that our most intimate and personally meaningful decisions about the conduct of our lives should be protected from governmental intrusion—is that it represents a way to prevent one religious or socio-ethnic group from imposing its moral codes on other people's most intimate life decisions.[37]

The Catholic Church, in concert with many evangelical Protestant churches, now seeks to maintain laws that prevent same-sex couples from gaining access to marriage, just as it long succeeded in maintaining laws that prevented married couples from using birth-control devices or ending unsuccessful marriages. The fact that it ultimately lost those earlier battles—not just in the court of law but in the court of public opinion, Catholic as well as non-Catholic—suggests that the momentum of historical change is against it, and that same-sex couples will someday achieve marriage equality. But nothing in history is inevitable. It is time now to explore the recent history that brought same-sex couples to the doors of Boston City Hall.

FOUR

Why Marriage
Became a Goal

*W*HEN THE FIRST gay political magazine, *ONE*, published a cover story on "homophile marriage" in June 1963, it drew attention to the large number of long-term gay relationships that gay people had taken to calling marriages. The article's author, Randy Lloyd, had complained that the magazine, like the straight press, paid disproportionate attention to the "single set," and he wanted to correct the situation. "Not everybody is suited for marriage," he admitted, "including plenty of heterosexuals." But there were plenty of homophile "married" couples, and he found a long-term commitment to another man a preferable way of life.

Lloyd complained about the antigay discrimination that made it difficult for men to meet. But he also admitted that he had been "amazed to discover" how many heterosexual couples accepted his marriage. They never talked about it—gays and straights usually weren't explicit with one another about such things in those days—but he thought the acceptance was real. "My real eye opener occurred when these heteros, with a cool nonchalance that made me feel woefully unsophisticated, started calmly pulling out from their social backgrounds, and introducing us to other homophile married couples!" This experience had led Lloyd to believe that "when society finally accepts homophiles as a valid minority with minority rights, it is going first of all to accept the married homophiles. We are, after all, the closest to their ideals."[1]

Although Lloyd didn't mention it, some gay "married couples" organized ceremonies to solemnize their commitment vows, and a handful found sympathetic clergy to officiate. At least since the 1920s, in fact, Harlem was noted for its elaborate gay and lesbian weddings, presided over by a few Baptist and storefront clergy. But most gay marriages were "customary" in the way that all marriages had once been: recognized as such by gay friends, and sometimes even heterosexual friends, once two people like Lloyd and his partner had established a home together and made clear their wish to be treated as a couple. The idea that such marriages might one day also be recognized by the state seems never to have occurred to him.

Less than a decade later, in the heady early days of gay liberation, a handful of same-sex couples filed lawsuits insisting that the state provide just such recognition. The courts dismissed their petitions as preposterous, and most lesbian and gay activists agreed. Indeed, the long and contentious gay and lesbian debate over the wisdom—and even the *desirability*—of pursuing marriage rights should disabuse anyone of the idea that there has ever been a single "gay agenda." Not until the 1990s did marriage become a widespread goal, and even then it received more support from lesbians and gay men at the grassroots level than from the major gay organizations. Even a decade ago, few would have predicted that San Francisco Mayor Gavin Newsom's February 2004 decision to start issuing marriage licenses would galvanize the community the way it did, prompting thousands of couples to stand in the rain waiting for their chance to wed. How, then, did marriage become an urgent goal for so many lesbians and gay men?

Early Gay Movements for Marriage Rights

From the earliest days of gay liberation, some activists demanded the right to marry. This may surprise some, who imagine that gay liberationists were united in denouncing marriage as a discredited patriarchal institution. But the messy complexity as well as the fervent politicization of the gay liberation years is part of what made them so generative and influential. Some liberationists rejected everything they associated with heterosexuality, including sex roles, marriage, and the family. But others insisted on their right to do everything heterosexuals did, from holding hands with a partner in public to getting married—either of which could seem a risky and even transformative event given the invisibility and hostility surrounding homosexuals in the early 1970s. Inspired by the millennial fervor that infused so much of the cultural activism of the late 1960s and 1970s, dozens of gay liberationists began the campaign for equal marriage rights by walking into county clerk offices to demand their license to marry.

On May 18, 1970, Mike McConnell, a librarian, and Jack Baker, a law student and Air Force veteran, applied for a marriage license from the county clerk in Minneapolis. Two months later Marjorie Jones and Tracy Knight filed a similar application in Louisville, Kentucky. In the following two years, more same-sex couples, some black and others white, ranging from the son of a noted socialite to two women on welfare, filed similar requests in Tampa, Hartford, Chicago, and Milwaukee. County clerks everywhere rejected these applications, but the two men in Minnesota and two women in Kentucky went on to file lawsuits contesting the clerks' decision.

McConnell and Baker's case received the most attention, including a three-page photo spread in a special issue of *Look* magazine on "The American Family" published in January 1971 (yet another sign of how anything seemed possible in the cultural turbulence of the early seventies). Baker and McConnell made it clear that they thought "Our getting married would be a political act with political implications," which would lead the state and society to recognize that their love was "as valid and deep as any heterosexual love." As Jack Baker put it, "Whatever rights straight people have, I want too." He went on to explain that "the institution of marriage has been used by the legal system as a distribution mechanism for many rights and privileges, [which] can be obtained only through a legal marriage." Allowing gay people to marry would give them "a new dignity and self-respect." It would also undermine sex roles. As they left the county clerk's office, a reporter waiting outside wanted to know who was going to be the wife. "We don't play those kinds of roles" came the reply.[2]

The lawsuits filed by the two couples noted that neither state law specified that a marriage could only be between a man and woman and insisted they had a basic civil right to marry. The college students from the local Gay Liberation Front who crowded the courtroom on the first day of the Louisville trial may have realized that the case wasn't going to go well when the judge told Tracy Knight that her beige pantsuit was "offensive to the court" before insisting that she go home and change into a dress. "She is a woman," the judge declared, "and she will dress as a woman in this court." Both cases were quickly dismissed. The courts had to concede that neither state law restricted marriage to a man and woman, but nonetheless concluded that marriage could not mean anything else. State legislatures took note. Beginning with Maryland, Texas, and Colorado in 1973, a total of fifteen states, mostly in the South and West, passed legislation in the next five years designed to limit marriage to heterosexual couples. Six of them did so in 1977, the year Miami's gay rights ordinance was overturned.[3]

A handful of radical gay liberationists were not the only gay people trying to get married. Performing such marriages was a central mission of the Metropolitan Community Church, a predominantly gay evangelical church founded in 1968 by the Rev. Troy Perry, a Pentacostalist minister from Florida who had been forced out of his church because of his homosexuality. A dozen people attended the first service, which Perry held in his living room in a suburb of Los Angeles on a Sunday morning in October 1968; within a few months, the church had grown to 150 and needed to rent a chapel for its services. Within three years, it had grown to more than 500 members, and the church had dedicated its first permanent sanctuary (the first building ever owned by a gay organization) at a service attracting more than a thousand people. New congregations had also been established in San Francisco, Chicago, and San Diego. By 1990, there were 240 congregations worldwide with a combined membership of 23,000. The MCC quickly became the largest lesbian, gay, bisexual, and transgender grassroots membership organization in history. Drawing its members largely from other evangelical churches, it was also the most racially diverse and working class in character.

From the beginning, the Metropolitan Community Church performed marriage ceremonies for same-sex couples who had been together for at least six months and had undergone pastoral counseling. In its first four years, the Los Angeles "Mother Church" alone performed more than 150 marriages. By the time Massachusetts legalized marriage, thirty-six years after the MCC's founding, church officials estimated that 85,000 marriages or holy unions had been performed at the denomination's hundreds of churches. Gay couples of faith also found other churches willing to solemnize their marriage vows or otherwise bless their commitments. *The Advocate* reported in 1972 that there were "mainline churches where such ceremonies are performed," although "the ministers often prefer to say merely that they are 'blessing' a union." Another new gay church, New York's Church of the Beloved Disciple, performed "holy unions." While the attitudes toward marriage waxed and waned in both the more radical and more cautious wings of the "mainstream" gay movement, marriage remained an aspiration for large numbers of lesbians and gay men.[4]

Gay Liberation, Lesbian Feminism, and Marriage

Still, support for marriage was a distinctly minority position in the lesbian and gay movement. Although some gay liberationists cheered the Minneapolis and Louisville couples on, others criticized them for "imitating meaningless, bad habits of our oppressors." "That isn't the freedom we want," wrote one critic in the New York newspaper *Gay Power.* "That isn't our liberation."[5] His editorial captured the dominant spirit among gay male liberationists (and many young heterosexuals as well), for whom "our liberation" centered instead on sexual liberation. From *Gay Power* to *The Advocate,* much of the early gay press urged men to overcome their sexual shame and to value the diverse pleasures and new friendships made possible by sexual experimentation with many partners. The gay press was full of ads for a burgeoning commercial sexual scene, from bars and dance clubs to porno bookstores and bathhouses. Old social patterns, in which former sexual partners often became friends and many men's sustaining emotional ties were with a small group of friends instead of a single partner, were newly celebrated.

Most lesbian feminist activists were even less interested in pursuing marriage rights. Most agreed that marriage was an inherently patriarchal institution, which played a central role in structuring the domination of women. As they sought to build a new women's culture shorn of patriarchal influence, many questioned monogamy and worked to construct new kinds of relationships and living patterns. Marriage—even between two women—was the last thing they wanted to advocate.

We shouldn't overstate the strength of any of these cultural or political tendencies in the 1970s. They were especially characteristic of young white lesbians and gay men living in certain places, although they had disproportionate political significance because those same people formed the core of the organized gay movement. The sexual revolution in San Francisco, New York, and a few other cities far outpaced that occurring in most of America. Most lesbians and gay men still looked for a steady relationship, and across the country, thousands of couples asked the MCC to bless their relationships as holy unions. Nevertheless, after an initial flurry of activity, marriage virtually disappeared as a goal of the movement outside of the ranks the MCC. The boundless optimism of the early 1970s about imminent social transformation faded in the face of entrenched discrimination and continuing hostility.

The handful of national organizations established in the 1970s—Lambda Legal Defense and Education Fund and the National Gay Task Force in 1973, the Gay Rights National Lobby (forerunner to the Human Rights Campaign) in 1976, the Lesbian Rights Project in 1977—and the burgeoning number of local organizations mostly ignored the issue, either because they were critical of marriage, saw it as a hopeless cause, or, most commonly, simply had other priorities. Instead of focusing on the rights of same-sex *couples*, gay politics at the time focused on securing the rights of *individuals* against discrimination in employment and on building *community* institutions and a collective culture.

Three developments in the 1980s increased the interest of lesbians and gay men in seeking legal recognition for their relationships. We've already chronicled the first: the dramatic growth in the visibility and acceptance of lesbians and gay men in some parts of the country and some segments of society. Their growing experience of equality began to make the fact that their relationships did not receive the same recognition given heterosexual relationships seem anomalous and unjust rather than part of the normal order of things. More important, however, were two searing experiences of the 1980s that forever impressed on lesbians and gay men the importance of securing their relationships: the devastating impact of AIDS and the astonishingly rapid appearance of what everyone soon called the lesbian baby boom. Neither development represents a "maturation" in the movement or in the individuals involved. But they resulted in the community's sudden, mass experience of two key stages in the life cycle that exert special pressure on any relationship: parenthood and death. Just as the post–World War II baby boom—a sudden jump in the birthrate that resulted from millions of individual couples simultaneously having more children than their parents and in a shorter period of time—had enormous consequences for postwar American culture, so the mass experience of child-rearing and death in the 1980s pushed lesbian and gay politics and culture in new directions. These experiences made people realize that no matter how accepted they were by their families, friends, and workmates, their relationships were still dangerously vulnerable.

The Impact of AIDS

AIDS confronted a generation of gay men with the fact that their relationships had no legal standing in the most ordinary, and profoundly consequential, ways. Within a stunningly short period of time—a few years in the 1980s—thousands of young men faced devastating illnesses and premature death. By 1988, seven years into the epidemic, 82,000 Americans had been diagnosed with AIDS, and 46,000 had already died. Few effective drug treatments were yet available, and 80 percent of those infected lived no more than two years after their diagnosis. Most people with AIDS were in their twenties, thirties, or forties; the median age was thirty-six. At that age, most people hadn't given much thought to control over medical decisions, estate planning, burials, or death. But suddenly neither they nor their partners or friends could escape such concerns. All at once, a generation of gay men had to contend with the lack of national health insurance in the United States because so many men lost their insurance when they became too sick to work. Couples whose relationships were fully acknowledged and respected by their friends suddenly had to deal with powerful institutions—hospitals, funeral homes, and state agencies—that refused to recognize them at all.

In the 1980s, the response of the gay communities in New York, San Francisco, Chicago, and other major cities to AIDS was strongly influenced by the fact that those communities had grown so quickly due to the massive gay migration of the 1970s. In the late 1980s, David Hansell directed the Gay Men's Health Crisis (GMHC) legal clinic that provided legal services to more than a thousand people with AIDS every year. As he discovered, longtime residents of New York were the men with AIDS most likely to be supported by friends. But most young men for whom he prepared wills and other legal documents had migrated to New York in the last ten years or so because they felt they had to get out of their hometowns. Some had found partners, most of whom stood by them when they became ill, but some of whom deserted them in fear and remorse. In the city's dance clubs, bathhouses, and cruising areas, many men had developed strong friendships with other gay men who rallied around them when they became ill. Others who had led more solitary lives, taking more advantage of the sexual than social possibilities offered by those venues, suddenly found themselves abandoned when they became sick. But thousands of gay men, as well as other men and women, gay and straight, rallied around them, volunteering to serve as their "buddies" and advocates. Ironically, the rapid growth of GMHC, ACT UP, and other AIDS service and activist organizations had a dramatic effect on the social organization of gay life, providing many more venues for the formation of friendships and ties to the larger community. The response to AIDS, in other words, simultaneously multiplied and strengthened the diverse forms of sociability and communal solidarity that had already developed and further reinforced the importance of relationships.[6]

In 1988, Rhonda Rivera, a resourceful attorney in Columbus, Ohio who had represented countless people with AIDS, provided a harrowing account of the dilemmas they and their partners faced.[7] At every stage, couples struggling to cope with a devastating illness found their problems magnified by the refusal of the medical profession or the state to recognize their relationship. Many of her clients, she reported, were estranged from their families because of their homosexuality and could not rely on them. Many relied instead on their friends or partners, but discovered that the state considered their partners to be no more than legal strangers. Because they were not "next of kin," hospitals could refuse them the right to visit their partners, did not need to consult with them or even inform them about treatment, and could not designate them to sign forms authorizing medical treatments even if they wanted to. The hospitalized partner could grant someone these rights with a medical power of attorney, and big-city hospitals that suddenly found themselves overwhelmed with AIDS cases often realized that it was in their own interest to accommodate the feisty friends who showed up to supervise and support their friends' medical care. But hospital staff in other parts of the country who were unaccustomed to AIDS cases or openly gay patients were not always so accommodating. Even a medical power of attorney could be disregarded in another state.

Gay men who had fled their hometowns and established new relationships and extended gay families in the gay meccas of New York and San Francisco discovered that hospitals and the state recognized the families they had fled over the informal new families they had created. David Hansell recalls, "A lot of people who migrated to New York were able to maintain good relations with their parents back home at the expense of concealing their gayness from them. They just never talked about that part of their life in New York." This meant that when the son got so sick that he couldn't conceal it from his parents anymore, the parents were simultaneously confronted with the news that their son had AIDS and that their son was gay. As Hansell noted, "Either thing would have been a shock to many parents, and the two together were especially hard to deal with. There was no opportunity for the parents to assimilate their son's gayness before they had to deal with the fact that he was dying. Many parents reacted by looking for someone to blame for doing this to their son, and very often they blamed his partner 'for making him gay' and for infecting him. It gave them a way to understand what had happened, but it exacerbated what would have been a difficult situation under any circumstances."

AIDS raised the emotionally charged question of who counted as family in the most profound ways. The biological family of an estranged son with AIDS was often content to let someone else take care of him. Conflicts were more likely to erupt over funeral arrangements and the estate. No matter how much a hospital might have cooperated with the partner during a man's illness, it usually felt it had no choice but to follow the wishes of the biological family when it came to the funeral, even when the family's plans went against the expressed wishes of the deceased. In Rivera's experience, this often meant that the funeral took place back in the hometown at the parents' church, even though their son may have rejected their religion, and that neither their son's gay life nor the cause of his death was mentioned in the obituary. Hansell recalled that many men wanted their ravaged bodies to be cremated, but Catholic and Jewish parents refused to allow this, since it wasn't a part of their tradition, and insisted on a burial instead. For many men dying from AIDS-related infections, and for the partners who saw them through to the end, making decisions about the disposition of their bodies gave them a small but invaluable sense of control over a situation that had spun almost entirely beyond their control. When parents refused to honor those wishes, the surviving partners found their inability to honor their loved one's last wishes exacerbated their sense of loss and distress. After attending the funeral at the parents' church, where the very existence of the partner was often not even admitted, they and their friends often organized alternative memorial services that celebrated the full life of their friend as they had known him. But as an official matter, there was simply no way of getting around the fact that their relationship had no legal standing.

Some survivors also found their homes and livelihoods threatened when their partners' families contested his will or claimed that jointly owned homes or property were legally theirs. If the couple had been able to marry, his partner would have automatically received his estate (or a substantial share of it, depending on the existence and age of children), even without a will. For years, older gay couples had tried to protect their partners by writing wills, but even before AIDS, hostile biological families had been remarkably successful in contesting such wills by charging that the homosexual partner had exerted "undue influence" over their deceased son or daughter.[8] Younger gay men suddenly forced to write wills found themselves in even greater jeopardy, since families often claimed that AIDS-related dementia had incapacitated their sons and invalidated the wills, even when couples had taken elaborate steps to certify mental health at the time of signing. Since the law required that an estate be distributed to a spouse, parents, or siblings, in that order, when someone died intestate (without a will), gay survivors knew they had a good chance of losing any suit filed against them, and often ended up giving up much of their inheritance in an out-of-court settlement.

The fact that gay couples had no legal status was even more devastating for poorer men, since they had so few resources to rely on when trying to establish their claims. Most of the gay men dying in the 1980s had few resources to begin with, and virtually none by the time they died, since they had often lost their jobs and insurance when they became too sick to work or their employer preemptively fired them. Often their "estate" consisted of little more than a record collection, a few personal possessions, some secondhand furniture, and, in New York, a lease to a rent-controlled apartment. But the same possessions were often all that the surviving partner had either, and represented the life they'd built together. A man could easily find himself locked out of his apartment after his partner died, since the police sealed an apartment after its occupant's death and usually refused to admit the survivor if his name hadn't been on the lease. The parents could get in when they came to town as the next of kin. But the partner often could not gain access to the apartment where he had nursed their son through his illness until the will naming him the beneficiary had gone through probate court. By then, the parents had often cleaned the apartment out.

The lack of a legally recognized family relationship also threatened a survivor's livelihood in other ways. Given the superheated New York City real estate market, many people never moved because they could only afford the rent-controlled apartment they had managed to get before rents went up in their neighborhood. If the lease was in the name of the man who was sick, the landlord could evict the survivor the day his lover died. If two men owned an apartment or house together, no relative contested the will, and the survivor received his partner's half of their home, he discovered that the IRS treated him very differently than a surviving spouse. If they had been married, only half of the value of the home would have been included in the gross estate for the purposes of calculating the estate tax, and in any case he would have paid no tax at because of the unlimited marital deduction. But in the case of unmarried partners, the IRS assumed the entire property belonged to the deceased unless his survivor could prove otherwise, usually by providing years of checks proving he had paid half of its costs.

The shattering realization that gay partners had no legal standing provided a powerful impetus to efforts to secure legal recognition. Those efforts and the sympathetic attention AIDS drew to the existence of committed gay couples played a key role in expanding the legal definition of family. One turning point came in 1989, when New York's highest court decided to recognize a gay couple as a family. Miguel Braschi had lived with his partner in the partner's rent-controlled apartment for ten years and had become his primary caretaker when the partner became ill. After his partner's death, the landlord sought to evict him so the rent could be raised for a new tenant, something forbidden in the case of a live-in spouse or child. Braschi was only one of many unmarried partners threatened with eviction. Many of those partners were ill themselves, at a time when homelessness and discrimination were growing problems for people with AIDS. In a landmark decision that all sides believed was deeply influenced by what Hansell called "the painful facts of AIDS," the New York Court of Appeals ruled that Braschi should be considered a family member for purposes of renter's succession rights. The "reality of family life" in the late twentieth century, the court ruled, was that functional, or informal, family relationships deserved recognition as well as those certified by the state. Henceforth, the state's Division of Housing and Community Renewal would need to expand its definition of family to include "two adult lifetime partners whose relationship is long term and characterized by an emotional and financial commitment and interdependence." The Division soon responded by issuing rules that expanded the definition of family even further. Braschi's attorney William Rubenstein hailed the rules as "the most far-reaching recognition of lesbian and gay relationships ever granted by any government agency in the United States."[9]

The attention AIDS drew to the devotion of committed gay couples like Miguel Braschi and his partner led other government agencies to recognize the reality of gay families. Shortly after the Braschi decision was greeted with acclaim by the New York press and legal establishment, Mayor Ed Koch announced that the domestic partners of city employees would henceforth be eligible for the bereavement leaves already available to spouses. A year later, San Francisco voters approved the establishment of a domestic partnership registry, after a debate profoundly shaped by the realities of AIDS and eight years after the measure had first been proposed. Within two years, six other cities had established similar registries and several more cities had begun offering health insurance or bereavement leave to the domestic partners of municipal employees.[10]

At the same time, AIDS activists joined other health care activists in advocating the creation of a national health insurance program that would make medical care a public right. In response to this activism and the growing public anxiety about the millions of Americans living without health care, Bill Clinton made solving the national health care crisis a central promise of his 1992 campaign. The ensuing defeat of his limited proposals for reform in 1994 demonstrated the power of physician groups and pharmaceutical industry lobbyists to stymie such efforts. This gave even more impetus to the campaign for domestic partnership policies, which might at least enable someone who lost his insurance when he became too sick to work to stay on his partner's health insurance.

The crisis provoked by AIDS did not immediately produce a groundswell of interest in securing equal marriage rights for lesbian and gay couples. Some activists opposed the idea on principle, and most others simply took it for granted that marriage would never be an option. Attorneys responding to the urgent needs of people with AIDS struggled to craft alternative legal arrangements—wills, health proxies, and domestic partnership registries—that might convey some of the rights and powers automatically granted by marriage. The early battles to protect the rights of people with AIDS and their partners nonetheless had an enduring impact on many gay people's thinking by abruptly confronting them with the legal inequality of their relationships.

The Lesbian Baby Boom

At the same time that gay men and their lesbian allies were confronting the problems faced by gay couples, a rapidly growing number of lesbian couples and smaller number of gay male couples confronted a related array of legal obstacles as they sought to raise children. Beginning in the early 1980s, people began to speak of a lesbian baby boom. Lesbians considering motherhood established a small "baby maybe" group in Washington, D.C., in 1982, whose members explored ways to have children, ranging from adoption to artificial insemination to intercourse with a male friend.[11] Beginning in the middle eighties, conferences for lesbians considering parenting were held in New York, San Francisco, Portland, and other cities; a conference held in Boston in 1988 on "Children in Our Lives" attracted 800 lesbians.

There were already many lesbians and gay men with children, but most of those children had been born when they were married or otherwise involved with people of the other sex, before they had come out as gay. Studies conducted in the 1990s established that one to nine million children had at least one lesbian or gay parent. But the lesbian baby boom of the 1980s represented something new: a generation of women who lived openly as lesbians and no longer felt obliged to marry a man in order to have a child. The complex legal issues raised by the lesbian baby boom provided another powerful impetus to the campaign to secure legal recognition of lesbian and gay families.[12]

The legal situation they faced was not auspicious. It was already difficult enough for lesbians and gay men who had become parents while in heterosexual marriages to keep custody of those children or even secure visitation rights in disputes with their former spouses. A growing number of such cases reached the courts in the 1970s and 1980s, and in case after case the courts took the custody of children away from a mother when her estranged husband had drawn her lesbianism to the court's attention, or denied visitation rights to a gay father. Such policies were challenged by attorneys from Lambda Legal Defense, the National Center for Lesbian Rights, and Gay & Lesbian Advocates & Defenders. They drew on studies by sociologists and child psychologists showing that children raised by homosexual parents were no different from children raised by heterosexual parents, and in particular were no more likely to be homosexual or emotionally maladjusted. Over the course of the 1980s and 1990s their efforts had considerable success in persuading courts to abandon rules that made it an irrebuttable presumption that a lesbian, gay, or bisexual parent was unfit for child custody or visitation.

By the mid-1990s, the courts in most states followed rules that required individualized assessment of plaintiffs' fitness as parents, including analysis of the effect of their being gay on the child. But as Julie Shapiro's 1996 study of custody cases around the country demonstrated, many courts continued to infuse those individualized assessments with their own prejudice against lesbians and gay men. As she discovered, courts were especially disapproving of lesbians and gay men who did not hide their sexuality from their children or from outsiders, and "disparagingly" characterized them as "flagrant," "notorious," or "'flaunting' their sexuality." A handful of widely publicized cases sent chills down the spines of gay parents everywhere. In the most widely publicized case (both *Time* and *People* ran stories on it), a Virginia court decided in 1993 to take Sharon Bottoms' two-year-old son away from her and give custody to Bottoms' own mother, because, as the trial court judge explained, her lesbian "conduct is illegal . . . a Class 6 felony in the Commonwealth of Virginia." In a chilling dismissal of the rights of lesbian mothers, he went on to declare "that it is the opinion of this Court that her conduct is immoral" and "renders her an unfit parent." Virginia's Supreme Court eventually rejected Bottoms' homosexuality as sufficient grounds for removing her child—but still upheld the trial court's decision terminating Sharon's parental rights.[13]

As in most matters gay, there were distinct regional variations in public and judicial attitudes. Lesbian or gay parents who lived with same-sex partners ran less (though still some) risk of losing their children in the Northeast and on the West Coast than comparable parents in the South and Midwest. As one Texas attorney commented in 1988, "unless [a mother] ended her open lesbian relationship I would have little chance of winning a custody trial."[14] Even when judges did not believe that a parent's homosexuality automatically disqualified her as a parent, they were likely to deny her custody because of the stigma they thought the children would endure if their peers learned the parent was gay. Some courts had used similar reasoning to remove children from the home of a divorced white mother who had married or moved in with a black man, a practice ruled unconstitutional by the Supreme Court only in 1984. In that case, *Palmore v. Sidoti*, Chief Justice Warren Burger ruled that "private biases [of the sort that might lead to the harassment of such a child] may be outside the reach of the law, but the law cannot directly, or indirectly, give them effect." But courts in many states continued to give legal effect to the private bias they assumed existed against lesbian and gay parents.[15]

The lesbian baby boom was concentrated in cities and regions where the courts were more likely to find gay parents to be acceptable, but their situation raised novel issues with which the courts had to grapple. Most commonly, the courts had to decide where to place a child when its biological mother died and one of her relatives contested the right of her surviving partner, the child's second mother, to continue to have a relationship with the child. In a number of cases that only exacerbated the worries of lesbian parents, courts granted custody to those relatives despite clear evidence that the child wished to remain with her surviving mother. Even in cases that were eventually decided in favor of the second mother, children were sometimes forced to live apart from her for months or even years. As the prominent lesbian rights lawyer Nancy Polikoff observed, "The harm these children suffered and are suffering was entirely predictable. . . . These children were up for grabs precisely because their surviving parents lacked legal status as parents and were vulnerable to anyone making a custody claim."

Equally vexing issues were raised when two women separated after one of them had given birth to a child whom both of them had raised. Since the women's relationship had no legal standing and the second mother had no legal relationship to the child, the usual rules governing custody disputes during a divorce did not apply. The second mother had little recourse if her estranged partner, the biological mother, simply refused to let her see the child. Beginning in the mid-1980s, some women turned to the courts to try to establish joint custody or visitation rights. The decisions were mixed. In the interest of encouraging the courts' recognition of lesbian families, Lambda, Gay & Lesbian Advocates & Defenders (GLAD), and other lesbian and gay litigation groups represented the second mother in several such cases. In gay families in which there was a clear agreement jointly to parent that the parties fulfilled, a growing number of courts allowed the second parent to secure custody or visitation rights and held them to corresponding child support obligations. The courts' authorization of such arrangements increased in part because research studies led numerous influential medical and mental health groups, including the American Academy of Pediatrics, to endorse nondiscriminatory standards. But it resulted as well from the simple fact that courts in Massachusetts, California, and other states where the lesbian baby boom was concentrated became more familiar with the realities of gay families.[16]

Gay couples could not count on any particular court to reach this conclusion, though. In response to the legal uncertainties following from the state's refusal to recognize their relationships, lesbian and gay parents and their lawyers developed a variety of strategies to protect their families. Many lesbian couples sought to protect themselves and their children by arranging for one partner to adopt the child who had been born to the other, which would grant her a secure legal relationship to the child. To do so, they had to gain access to a second-parent adoption procedure that had been developed to allow stepparents to establish a legal relationship with the children of their spouses. In the mid-1980s, some states began to allow this, and twenty years later, almost half the states allowed second-parent adoptions by gay and lesbian partners, a legal mechanism that became part of the federal Uniform Adoption Act. Gay male couples continued to face distinctive legal obstacles, since they first needed to persuade the courts to allow one gay man to adopt a child, then to permit joint adoption by *two* unmarried men whose relationship did not have the legal standing of marriage.

Some gay parents who took advantage of the new legal procedures worried about how much security they provided. As one woman in Massachusetts who later decided to get married explained, "It was a huge influence, the fact that we had to go through second-parent adoption to be recognized as the legal parent of our own children. My partner and I each had a child biologically, and so we each had to adopt the other's biological child. And there was about a six month period for each child when one of us was not a legal parent to one of our children, and that was a terrible thing."

The lesbian baby boom, as much as AIDS, led growing numbers of lesbians and gay men to start thinking the unthinkable: that lesbians and gay men needed and deserved the rights and protections of marriage. And like AIDS, the wrenching legal issues it raised educated the courts about gay families and the damage being done to them by legal discrimination. In the 1980s and 1990s, courts in New York, Massachusetts, Vermont, California, and elsewhere encountered gay men who nursed their partners through a devastating illness, and then were forced onto the streets because they had no claim to their established family home. They met children who were devastated when they lost both of their mothers after one of them died and her relatives took the child away from the other.

The publicity surrounding these cases educated the public and state legislatures as well as the courts. In Massachusetts, for instance, the courts ruled in 1993 that same-sex unmarried parents could adopt a child together. The fact that both parents now had legal standing meant that other institutions had to recognize them both as parents, whether that meant granting them access to a child's school records or recognizing them on the child's insurance forms. Other parents saw them volunteering as tutors at the school or being elected to office in the PTA. Gay families became part of the social fabric in Massachusetts and like-minded states, no matter how invisible they remained in other parts of the country. By the end of the nineties, polls showed continuing opposition to the idea that same-sex couples should be allowed to marry. But they also showed growing support for the right of lesbian and gay couples to adopt children. The world was changing.

Sharon Kowalski and the Vulnerability of Lesbian and Gay Relationships

AIDS and the baby boom altered many gay people's thinking about their relationships. But so, too, did a handful of frightening and highly publicized cases that showed how vulnerable gay couples could be. Above all, the experience of Sharon Kowalski and her partner Karen Thompson brought the vulnerability of lesbian and gay couples home to everyone. In

1983, Sharon and Karen had been lovers for four years and led a quiet life in the home they owned together in St. Cloud, Minnesota. They had named one another beneficiaries on their insurance policies, but had not thought to make other legal arrangements. Few couples did in those days, and they were only in their thirties. They had not come out to their families or colleagues. Karen, a teacher, was afraid she might be fired.

Disaster struck when Sharon was in a severe automobile accident that left her paralyzed and unable to speak. When Karen raced to the hospital, the staff refused to let her see her partner in intensive care for two hours, until she persuaded them that she was acting as the emissary of Sharon's parents, who had not yet arrived. They let her see Sharon for five minutes. Once he arrived, the father refused to listen to her suggestions for Sharon's treatment, and since he was next of kin, the doctors turned to him for approval. Several weeks later, after staying with Karen during their visits, the parents questioned their relationship and told them they planned to move Sharon to a different facility. After Karen wrote the parents to try to explain the women's relationship, they refused to believe their daughter was a lesbian, charged that Thompson had perverted her, and took steps to keep them from seeing one another. After the father won guardianship in 1985, he moved the daughter away and left her with virtually no care. Karen finally won the right to be reunited with Sharon and to take care of her, but only after a court battle that stretched on until 1991. The case was seared into lesbian and gay consciousness as the gay press chronicled every stage of Karen's long battle to bring her partner home. For several years some Gay Pride marches were led by an empty wheel-chair. Because the case struck so close to home for gay couples, it forced many people to think about the unthinkable: that they could be separated from their loved ones unless they found ways to secure their relationships.[17]

Horror stories like these prompted more lesbian and gay couples to prepare the legal documents that might protect them from such catastrophes. Like most heterosexuals, though, most lesbians and gay men did not make these legal arrangements, either because they just never got around to it, no matter how good their intentions, or because they could not afford it. A full set of the documents necessary to approximate the protections provided by marriage could cost several thousand dollars; a marriage license might cost $25. However onerous marriage had once seemed to some, its advantages became clearer to many. In one stroke, it provided a range of protections to couples—from hospital visitation rights and legal guardianship in case of catastrophic accident or illness, to children's security in families and principles to guide the dissolution of a relationship. People could always prepare other documents to tailor at least some marriage rules to their own situation: granting medical power of attorney to someone else, for instance, or signing a prenuptial agreement that would govern property distribution in case of divorce. But marriage would provide them with a standard set of protections. And given the expense of other legal documents, marriage was the only way many poorer couples could afford such protections at all.

Marriage also offered a degree of security that no other set of legal documents could match. Karen Thompson and

Sharon Kowalski might not have had to spend six years apart if they had executed a medical power of attorney before Sharon's accident. But like most young couples, they never expected an accident to shatter their lives. And if Sharon's father had found the "right" judge, he might still have been able to trump such a document by virtue of his status as the "next of kin." As most attorneys preparing such documents tell a couple, they help a lot. But they're no guarantee.

People's visceral understanding of this grew as other stories circulated. Not stories they read about in the papers, or heard about at rallies, but stories that involved their friends. Two women waiting to get their marriage licenses at Cambridge City Hall told one such story. A lesbian couple they knew, Michele Granda and Kate Hogan, had been on vacation in the British Virgin Islands two years earlier. One day Michele and Kate had gone kayaking in a bright yellow two-seater. A 39-foot motorboat suddenly appeared out of nowhere and ran directly over their kayak; Michele managed to get out of the way, but Kate bled to death within hours. A life-shattering experience quickly became even more nightmarish. The women had been together for twelve years, shared a home, were embraced by their families. But the hospital would not let Michele stay with Kate in the emergency room as she died. The American Consulate read about the accident in the papers and contacted Michele the next morning. They wondered if she had a telephone number for Kate's father, so they could contact the next of kin. One of her friends remembered, "There were a lot of issues because they weren't married. If they had been married, the legal recourse would have been incredibly straightforward, and it wasn't."

The effect on their friends was sobering. "I think we had all thought, we're pretty successful in our careers, a lot of us were lawyers," mused one. "We thought we were pretty secure. We thought, we have wills, we're fine. But it's not true." Kate and Michele had every document you could imagine. And when this happened, they didn't count for a thing. "You can do some things" with those documents, the friend continued, "but you cannot replicate marriage." The lack of recognition was almost as troubling as the legal issue: "At the funeral service, the priest didn't even recognize her partner of twelve years. He talked about her father, he talked about her brother, and he did not talk about her partner. He couldn't have done that if she had been her spouse." As a feminist, she still had a lot of criticisms of the way heterosexual women were treated in marriage. But she and her partner were going to get married. They were going to protect themselves as much as possible.

Jon Davidson, senior counsel in Lambda Legal's Los Angeles office, tells a similar story in explaining one of the reasons he's an ardent advocate of gay couples' right to marry. Bill Flanigan and Robert Daniel, who'd lived together in San Francisco for five years, were on a trip to visit Robert's relatives in Washington, D.C., when Robert became very ill and was rushed to the hospital. Although the two men had signed all the appropriate documents and registered as domestic partners in California, the staff at the University of Maryland Medical System told Bill he could not see Robert in the shock trauma center because he was not Robert's family. Only when Robert's mother and sister arrived from out of town, four hours later, was Bill allowed in, with them, to see Robert. By then, Robert was no longer conscious, his eyes were taped shut, and—against Robert's wishes, which he had shared with Bill—a breathing tube had been inserted down Robert's throat. Because they were never allowed to marry and because anything less than marriage is still seen as less significant, Bill and Robert never got to say good-bye to one another.

The Campaign for Domestic Partnership

Stories like this reminded people of the fragility of life and impressed on them the legal vulnerability of their relationships. As a result, more couples hired lawyers to prepare wills, medical powers of attorney, and other legal documents that promised to provide *some* security to their relationships. People also took up the campaign for domestic partnership in earnest, and in the early 1990s there were major breakthroughs. In 1992, the software company Lotus became the first publicly traded company to offer domestic partnership benefits, and others soon followed. When Stanford and the University of Chicago both announced in December 1992 that they would offer the same benefits to the same-sex partners of faculty, staff, and students that they already offered married couples, it opened the floodgates and scores of other schools soon followed.

Companies' initial fears that the incidence of AIDS among gay men would jack up their health care costs or even bankrupt their health care budgets proved unfounded. Indeed, as universities, companies, and municipal governments soon learned, domestic partnership policies usually generated favorable press and tremendous goodwill among their employees at little cost, and even gave them a competitive edge in recruiting top talent. On May 17, 2004, the day Massachusetts began issuing marriage licenses to same-sex couples, almost half of the country's Fortune 500 companies offered health benefits to same-sex partners, including Coca-Cola and the big three automakers. Altogether, more than 7,000 employers offered health insurance and other benefits to the same-sex domestic partners of their employees, including ten state governments and more than 125 municipalities and counties. Only four companies and three governmental units had done so in 1986. Even President George W. Bush signed legislation—named after the gay fire department chaplain who died while administering last rites at the World Trade Center on September 11, 2001—allowing death benefits to be paid to the domestic partners of firefighters and police officers who die in the line of duty.[18]

More than half of the Fortune 500 employers—and more than two-thirds of municipal governments—providing such benefits made them available to unmarried heterosexual couples as well as gay couples. Domestic partnership programs could be especially important to lower-paid workers. Gay people, like heterosexuals, tend to get involved with people like themselves. Relatively few professionals need to use domestic partnership to provide their partners with health insurance, for instance, because most professionals are involved with other professionals who already have health insurance through their own jobs. (Although even they could need it if one stayed home with children.) Workers in the lowest ranks of the workforce were more likely to be involved with people who were either unemployed or held jobs not providing benefits.

Domestic partnership thus represented an important advance for many gay couples, especially those who were the least secure financially. Of course, many activists wondered why someone needed to have a domestic partner with health benefits in order to get health insurance herself. Domestic partnership did not change the most fundamental inequities and shortcomings of the American health care system. But it did end some inequities. By the 1990s, some 30 percent of a typical employee's compensation came in the form of benefits, and gay workers and other unmarried workers whose partners did not receive the same benefits provided to the spouses of their married heterosexual colleagues were not earning equal compensation for the same work. Domestic partnership policies at least began to bring a degree of equality to the workplace.

The other trouble was that the rapid spread of domestic partnership policies in the 1990s solved only some of the problems facing gay couples. No domestic partnership policy could provide hospital visitation rights, or social security benefits, or the pension protections available to married couples. Nor did the federal government treat domestic partnership benefits the same way it treated the equivalent benefits received by married couples. While an employee's domestic partner could now get health insurance, the employee was taxed on her employer's contribution to the coverage—something the IRS did not impose in the case of married couples. What was worse, the federal ERISA regulations governing many retirement programs made it impossible for an unmarried same-sex partner to receive the same pension benefits that a husband or wife would receive when their partner died. Even after thousands of companies established domestic partnership programs, federal policies still required the private welfare system to discriminate against same-sex couples who could not get married. Domestic partnership policies seemed like an enormous step forward at the time, and they were. But as the people who used them soon came to realize, they were anything but equal even in the limited area of workplace benefits. The federal government continued to treat unmarried couples as second-class citizens.

The Renewal of Community Debate

For a long time, though, few activists thought of trying to secure marriage as a way to overcome at least some of these inequities. In the Reagan years, the *Bowers* years, and the early AIDS years, it seemed preposterous to most activists that the courts or public would ever be willing to grant such rights. But at the 1987 March on Washington, some 2,000 lesbian and gay couples showed their support for marriage rights by participating in a mass wedding on the steps of the IRS. In the next several years, the willingness of a few courts and municipal governments to offer limited recognition to lesbian and gay couples prompted a renewed debate over marriage among gay rights attorneys and other activists. The debate only intensified in the mid-1990s as a series of court rulings suggested winning marriage rights might actually be in grasp.

A full accounting of the gay debate over the desirability of marriage is beyond the scope of this book. It was fierce and wide-ranging. It reflected, and to some extent became captive to, a series of emerging divisions within the distinct but overlapping feminist and lesbian, gay, bisexual, and transgender movements.

In the late 1980s, the marriage debate began to divide lesbian feminists who had previously worked together on other issues. Many feminists such as the law professor and influential legal activist Nancy Polikoff argued that lesbians and gay men should continue to seek alternatives to marriage (as, indeed, growing numbers of heterosexuals did). In their view, marriage was inescapably linked to its historic role as a central institution perpetuating male domination over women. Demanding inclusion into marriage would betray the principles of feminism both by ratifying that regime and locking same-sex couples into it. It was more important to fight for domestic partnership policies and child custody policies that provided alternatives to marriage rather than reinforcing its dominance. Other feminists, such as the founder of the ACLU's Lesbian and Gay Rights Project, Nan Hunter, regarded marriage as a more flexible institution, which had been profoundly changed since the 1970s and would be changed again by the inclusion of same-sex couples. She strongly supported the campaign for domestic partnership policies, but warned that securing them alone would "create a second-class status rather than an alternative, leaving lesbian and gay couples still excluded from marriage by force of state law; in no sense, without a marriage option available, could they be assumed to be 'choosing' partnership." Yet others warned that marriage played such a pervasive role in allocating recognition, rights, and protections that it would never be equalled by domestic partnership.[19]

Especially among gay men, the debate was shaped by both the soul-searching produced by the AIDS crisis and the growth of a self-proclaimed conservative gay political movement (whose very existence was a sign of how much the place of lesbians and gay men in American society and politics had changed). AIDS led some men to challenge the dominant sexual ethic that had taken shape during the sexual revolution of the late 1960s and 1970s, which saw monogamy as a linchpin of the culture of sexual shame and stressed not just the pleasures of sexual experimentation but the role it could play in self-exploration and community building. Many men who advocated a new ethic of monogamy embraced marriage as one means of giving it life and institutional form. If the original gay advocates of marriage had seen it as an instrument of gay liberation and social transformation, many of marriage's most famous advocates in the early 1990s, such as the *New Republic* editor Andrew Sullivan, saw marriage as a means of mainstreaming gay culture. The writer Jonathan Rauch argued that marriage was a positive good because it would "civilize" gay men and increase the pressure on men to retreat from the sexual culture of the seventies by increasing the stigma unmarried gay men faced. Such arguments produced a strong reaction from Michael Warner and other gay men and lesbians who felt making marriage a central movement goal (or even supporting it) would dishonor the innovative forms of intimacy that had taken shape in queer culture. Stigmatizing such alternatives was the last thing they wanted.[20]

If one side embraced marriage's symbolic power to assimilate gay couples into the mainstream of American life, another side resisted it as an assimilationist retreat from the radical aspirations of gay liberation. The debate revealed genuine and growing disagreements among gay activists, but it also often seemed to me to misconstrue the likely significance of securing marriage in part because of the way it used the term "assimilation." Historians once used the term to describe the process by which Mexicans, Asians, European Catholics, and other immigrants were absorbed into American culture and became indistinct from it, as they shed all signs of their difference from the national norm. Although that framework still underpins the debate over gay assimilation, it has been refashioned by theorists of ethnicity, who recognize that even as immigrants were reshaped by their incorporation into American culture, so too was American culture.[21] Securing marriage will have significant symbolic implications, but they will be more complex than the debate over assimilation usually allows. Just as problematic, neither side in the assimilation debate paid much attention in the 1990s to the tangible rights, benefits, and protections conferred by marriage. That would soon change.[22]

So too would the political context for the debate. In the 1980s and early 1990s, few people who were debating the desirability of marriage so fervently actually thought there was much prospect of it becoming available to gay couples anytime soon. A series of court decisions in the 1990s and early 2000s changed that. By making marriage seem a real possibility for the first time and by provoking a massive conservative reaction, the court decisions intensified the gay debate but also shifted its center of gravity. More and more activists and non-activists came to believe that both the security and recognition that marriage provided were worth fighting for.

From Hawaii to Massachusetts

The stage for the national marriage debate was set by the changing character of marriage, the changing circumstances of gay life, and the changing place of gay people in American society. AIDS and the lesbian baby boom both made gay people more conscious of the vulnerability of their relationships and the need to secure them, and made many heterosexuals more sympathetic to the needs and lived realities of their gay friends and neighbors. The continuing attacks on gays made their need for protection even greater, while the dramatic growth of many heterosexuals' acceptance of gay people made securing some form of legal protection possible. Lesbian and gay couples continued to press the major gay legal organizations to help them get married. But it was the vision of a few key legal strategists and the decisions of a few state courts that took the issue to the next level.

Mary Bonauto was the second full-time attorney ever hired by Gay & Lesbian Advocates & Defenders (usually called GLAD), the small Boston-based gay legal public interest group that played the same role for New England that the far larger organization, Lambda Legal, did elsewhere. Massachusetts had just become the second state in the nation to pass a gay rights law, and GLAD hired her to make sure that it was enforced. She remembers three of the requests for legal representation she found on her desk on her first day in the office,

March 19, 1990. A high school teacher was being harassed, a lesbian couple wanted to jointly adopt their daughter, and a lesbian couple from western Massachusetts who'd been together for ten years wanted to get married. "I said yes to the first two," she recalled, "and no to the third." Bonauto was already committed to gay marriage, but thought it was the wrong time to push the issue: "Our relationships with each other were not acknowledged at any level. We didn't have any domestic partnership ordinances in Massachusetts, and our rights vis-à-vis our children were extremely limited." The courts—and the public—needed to be better educated about gay families before they were asked to recognize them as equal.

About the same time, three gay couples in Hawaii, including Nina Baehr and Genora Dancel, were also making the rounds looking for lawyers willing to help them get married. Both the ACLU and Lambda turned them down, but Dan Foley, the former director of Hawaii's ACLU, agreed to take the case. Evan Wolfson, an attorney at Lambda who was already known in gay legal circles as a strong advocate of marriage rights, persuaded his boss to let him work on the case behind the scenes. Eventually he became co-counsel, and the case catapulted him into a central role in the marriage movement.

Marriage had been a burning issue for Wolfson since his days as a Harvard law student a decade earlier. "It was just very clear to me that we needed to be talking about marriage," he recalled, because it's the "central social and legal institution of this and virtually every other society, and you can't say that you're for equality and then acquiesce in our exclusion from it." He believed it also had a larger significance, because marriage provided "a vocabulary in which non-gay people talk about larger important questions—questions of love and commitment and dedication and self-sacrifice and family, but also equality and participation and connectedness." He believed that "in claiming that vocabulary we make it easier for non-gay people to understand who we are."

To everyone's astonishment, the Hawaii plaintiffs came within an inch of winning full marriage rights. After a trial court's dismissal of the case, the Hawaii Supreme Court ruled in 1993 that the marriage ban presumptively violated the state's Equal Rights Amendment, and remanded the case to the trial court to determine if there was a "compelling state interest" in denying the couples' right to marry.

The Hawaii decision was a historic breakthrough that far surpassed the dreams of gay litigators and activists and "unleashed a tremendous energy amongst gay and non-gay people on our side," Wolfson recalled. He hit the road, urging other movement groups and allies to join in the campaign for marriage. But the case also reinforced some lawyers' fears about the consequences of a "premature" marriage victory. The lower court waited three years, until September 1996, before beginning the trial on the state's arguments. On the first day of the trial the U.S. Senate voted 85–14 for the Defense of Marriage Act (DOMA), which the House had passed that summer by a vote of 342–67. The act provided a federal definition of marriage as the union of one man and one woman and declared that no other state needed to give "full faith and credit" to same-sex marriages performed in another state. It also denied federal benefits to such married couples. A coalition of traditional family values groups had campaigned heavily for the law and insisted every Republican presidential candidate pledge his support for it. President Clinton, not having forgotten how the gays-in-the-military issue roiled the first months of his administration, signed it in the dead of night.

As it turned out, DOMA was enacted to counteract something that never happened in Hawaii. The trial court ruled in support of the gay couples, but the state appealed to the state Supreme Court, which sat on the case another three years. The state legislature voted to put a constitutional amendment on the November 1998 ballot to invalidate the court's anticipated ruling in support of gay couples. National conservative groups poured money into the state, and gay activists lost the vote 69 to 29 percent. When an Alaska trial court judge ruled that same year that banning same-sex marriages was unconstitutional, the decision was quickly overturned by a similar constitutional amendment.

Disappointed but undaunted, Wolfson still considered the Hawaii case to be a turning point. It showed that marriage could be won and moved the issue into the center of national debate, for gays and non-gays alike. As he travelled the country during the period of what he called the "Hawaii hope," he was stunned to see the excitement and enthusiasm unleashed by the original decision, often on the part of people who had not been involved in gay organizations before. When State Senator Pete Knight tried to push legislation banning same-sex marriages through the California legislature, it generated more progay mail than any other gay legislative issue ever had. But the fierce resistance to the Hawaii decision was equally stunning. Fifteen legislatures enacted "state DOMAs" in 1996. When Knight put a "Protection of Marriage Initiative" on the 2000 ballot, it passed with 61 percent of the vote. Many activists worried that the suddenly inescapable focus on marriage was diverting attention from other issues and that the reaction it provoked would undermine other gains.

The Hawaii marriage case showed it was possible to persuade a court that the ban on gay couples marrying was an unconstitutional affront to equality. But it also showed that a majority of the public remained decidedly unconvinced. In 1997, as the Hawaii case dragged on and state DOMAs multiplied, Mary Bonauto and two Vermont lawyers, Beth Robinson and Susan Murray, decided it was time to file a new lawsuit that would renew the conversation.

The intervening years had only strengthened Bonauto's conviction that marriage was worth fighting for. Along with the cases and negotiations she had initiated to increase the enforcement of Massachusetts's antidiscrimination law, extend domestic partnership benefits, and to combat antigay violence, she had won numerous cases involving adoption, child visitation rights after a lesbian couple separated, and other family issues. She knew that some gay activists and attorneys believed the movement should continue to seek access to such rights and benefits outside of marriage, but came to believe this was a recipe for going "along one painful step by painful step, trying to say we should have access to this protection or that protection. I felt like our litigation options were limited. With most of the rights of marriage, there's an explicit rule, that the benefit, protection, or responsibility is available only to a 'spouse.' And in the end the only way we'd be able to end the denial of those protections would be to become spouses." Gaining access to marriage wasn't going to resolve all of the problems gay people faced, but it would decisively solve a number of them.

At the same time, she was acutely aware of the gay debate over the desirability of marriage. She continued to get requests for representation from couples all over New England who wanted to get married, but she also participated in national discussions among lawyers who were nearly all convinced that the right to marriage could not yet be won. She was also well aware of feminist and queer critiques of marriage. "I understand those perspectives," she commented. "But in the end, when you actually puzzle it through and you see the number of rights associated with marriage that are otherwise categorically denied, when you see the number of people who say they want to choose this, when you see that marriage has become a gender-neutral institution and an institution of legal equality, some of these critiques don't seem so compelling anymore." Her concern was that there should be a variety of family models available to people, and that all people, including lesbians and gay men, should have a choice among them.

Vermont seemed like a place where they might win that choice. It was a tolerant state with a strong gay grassroots movement committed to the marriage issue; the Vermont Freedom to Marry Task Force had been organized in 1995. Robinson, Murray, and Bonauto filed the case, *Baker v. Vermont*, on behalf of three couples in July 1997. In December 1999 the Vermont Supreme Court ruled that it was unconstitutional to deny the benefits of marriage to same-sex couples and directed the legislature to remedy the situation. Five months later Governor Howard Dean signed legislation establishing "civil unions" for same-sex couples, which provided some of the legal benefits of marriage, but not the name.

A decade earlier such state recognition of gay couples would have been unthinkable, but the lawyers were dismayed by the outcome. Civil unions provided none of the many federal rights and benefits that marriage did—from social security to pension protections and tax considerations—and constituted a separate, unequal category for some couples compared to others. "One of the main protections that comes with marriage," Wolfson insisted, "is the word marriage, which brings clarity and security that is simply not replaceable by any other word or by a sheaf of documents."

In April 2001, a year after Vermont enacted civil unions, Bonauto filed the *Goodridge* marriage case in Boston. Massachusetts was as strategic a choice as Vermont. Its Supreme Judicial Court had already shown that it took gay family issues and antigay discrimination seriously. According to Bonauto, "You have to look at the law and the track record of the judiciary. Is it a judiciary that has dealt with gay people before, and gay and lesbian families? How much does it wrestle with its constitution, and what equality means, what liberty means?" The SJC was such a court. In the 1990s it had ruled to allow an unmarried couple to jointly adopt a child, to honor a contract between two unmarried people when they separated, and to grant child visitation rights to a woman in a lesbian family after its dissolution. They could almost count on losing at the trial court level (as they did), but it was clear that the SJC would at least give their appeal a fair hearing.

Although Massachusetts was a very Catholic state with a conservative religious hierarchy opposed to gay rights, its legislature had enacted pioneering antidiscrimination measures. It was also a tolerant state, which made it easier for lesbian and gay families in every community to be open with their neighbors. As Bonauto saw it, that meant that "during the course of the case, as the right wing attack set in, people would be able to evaluate for themselves whether or not the awful things that were being said about gay people were really true about the gay people they knew." That would also matter if they won the case. No one could forget how the Hawaii victory had been lost. In Massachusetts, it would take at least two years for a constitutional amendment to reach the ballot. The Freedom to Marry Coalition and other grassroots organizations were ready to take the case to the people.

GLAD's lawsuit argued that the exclusion of Hillary and Julie Goodridge and the other six plaintiff couples from marriage violated their liberty and due process rights and violated the state constitutional guarantee of equality. GLAD called for the court to subject the marriage ban to a heightened form of judicial review, or "strict scrutiny," because it was a form of sex discrimination (since it denied a woman the right to marry someone whom a man could marry). It also discriminated against lesbians and gay men. At the very least, GLAD argued, there was no rational basis for the ban. "As a matter of logic and common sense," none of the interests the state claimed were protected by the ban were actually advanced by the ban. It was irrational and "arbitrary."[23]

The state defended the marriage ban by arguing it served a number of compelling interests. Its case repeated the usual conservative arguments made against same-sex marriage, and the trial court accepted them. But when the case reached the Supreme Judicial Court, GLAD countered each of those arguments with the backing of some of the state's and nation's most prestigious professional and scientific authorities. In a sign of how times had changed, numerous professional associations submitted amicus briefs (or friend-of-the-court briefs) to the SJC designed to expose every argument made against same-sex marriage as misinformed, a selective rule just for gay people, or the product of prejudice rather than research.

Has procreation long been recognized as the central purpose of marriage, as the trial court ruled when it rejected GLAD's case? Not according to the authors of the most widely used treatise on Massachusetts family law. They explained in their friend-of-the-court brief that neither the ability nor willingness to procreate has ever been a condition for entering a marriage, nor has the inability to have children been a legal basis for ending a marriage. Statutory law and case law both showed that marriage instead established certain relational rights and obligations, which were designed to "support individuals' expectations of emotional and sexual intimacy, vows of fidelity and commitment and sharing of economic assets and support." Although procreation was well-established as a fundamental right, people did not have to be married to procreate, and they did not have to procreate or even be capable of procreation to marry.

The lower court had ruled that it was "rational to limit marriage to opposite-sex couples who, theoretically, are capable of procreation." But as the family law scholars argued, the state

had never applied this criterion to ban marriages, by, for instance, prohibiting "post-menopausal women from marrying,
even though they cannot bear children." Nor were the sterile
or the incarcerated prohibited from marrying, even though
they, too, were theoretically incapable of procreation. Nor had
the state ever been willing to annul marriages or grant fault-
based divorces on the grounds that one spouse was infertile. In
fact, the state supported the decision of infertile heterosexual
couples and gay couples alike to bring children into their families through adoption or the use of reproductive technology.[24]
The state, in short, had never recognized the ability to procreate as a rational basis for determining who could marry.

But, in fact, many lesbian and gay couples do raise children. Is there a rational basis, as the state alleged, for believ-
ing "that the optimal setting for raising children is a two-
parent family with one parent of each sex?" No, according to
a brief submitted by the Massachusetts Psychiatric Society,
the American Psychoanalytic Association, the National Association of Social Workers, and other professional associations
concerned with the well-being of children, along with the
chairs of the pediatrics departments at several Boston-area
hospitals.[25] "Every medical, psychological, and child-welfare
organization to have addressed the topic," they reported, "has
concluded what the plaintiffs know from their own family experiences: children of same-sex parents are as healthy, happy,
and well adjusted as their peers." This consensus was confirmed by a review of more than fifty peer-reviewed studies
conducted over a generation. The American Academy of Pediatrics, for one, had issued a formal report documenting that
"children who grow up with 1 or 2 gay and/or lesbian parents

fare as well in emotional, cognitive, social, and sexual functioning as do children whose parents are heterosexual."[26] In 1995, after conducting a comprehensive review of research studies, the American Psychological Association concluded that "not a single study has found children of gay or lesbian parents to be disadvantaged in any significant respect relative to children of heterosexual parents."[27] But they were disadvantaged, the brief commented, by the fact "that the State will not allow their parents to marry."

But weren't lesbian and gay couples less stable than heterosexual couples? It was hard to be conclusive on this question, given the absence of reliable statistics on gay couples. But the most highly regarded studies showed that "'many if not most' gays and lesbians live in stable, committed long-term relationships because they 'desire for an enduring love relationship with a partner of the same gender.'"[28] One study had shown that of couples together for ten years, breakup rates were 4 percent for married heterosexual couples, 4 percent for gay men, and 6 percent for lesbians. Other comparative studies showed virtually no difference in the quality of relationships between gay couples and heterosexual couples.[29] In any case, heterosexuals were not prevented from marrying because half of their first marriages ended in divorce.

Both Bonauto and the friends of the court pointed to the seven couples who were the plaintiffs in the case. The couples owned homes together, merged their finances, owned their personal property jointly, and named each other beneficiaries on their insurance and retirement policies. Richard Linnell and Gary Chalmers, who had been a couple for thirteen years, had moved into Richard's family home at his mother's request. Hillary and Julie Goodridge, together for fourteen years, had a five-year-old daughter, Annie, and both volunteered on committees at her school. Maureen Brodoff and Ellen Wade, together for twenty years, were raising a twelve-year-old daughter; Maureen had been constantly at Ellen's side after she was diagnosed with cancer. Mike Horgan and Ed Balmelli, together eight years, both came from large families in central Massachusetts. They vacationed with their siblings' families; Ed's mother called Mike her son-in-law.

As GLAD wrote, "because there is no legal recognition for their committed relationship," the partners in these couples "are not considered to have any legal relationship to each other. These Plaintiffs are denied on a daily basis the legal and social status of a marital relationship, as well as the protections, benefits and obligations—financial, legal, emotional and others—afforded to married couples."[30] This rendered them second-class citizens. And there was no rational basis for it.

The Supreme Judicial Court delayed its decision for months longer than anyone anticipated. But on November 18, 2003, it ruled in the plaintiffs' favor. Its ruling seemed to embrace some of the other arguments GLAD had made, but it ultimately based its decision on the fact that there simply was no rational basis for the ban. Writing for the majority, Chief Justice Margaret Marshall declared that

> The Massachusetts Constitution affirms the dignity and equality of all individuals. It forbids the creation of second-class citizens. In reaching our conclusion we have given full deference to the arguments made by the Commonwealth. But

it has failed to identify any constitutionally adequate reason for denying civil marriage to same-sex couples.[31]

Hawaii's Supreme Court had returned its case to the trial court, where it died a slow death. Vermont's Supreme Court had offered the legislature a way to remedy the problem without extending marriage to gay couples. But the Massachusetts court made it clear that a separate and unequal remedy such as civil unions would not suffice. It insisted that the state start issuing marriage licenses to same-sex couples 180 days later, on May 17. As it turned out, that was the fiftieth anniversary of *Brown v. Board of Education*.

Reading the decision on the courthouse plaza the day it was released "took my breath away," Bonauto recalled. "They accepted liberty and equality as bedrock promises of the government to the people and made no exception for same-sex couples. They spoke with heart in recognizing the 'deep and scarring hardship' as well as the enormous practical difficulties when the government denies us marriage rights. They spoke the truth and rebutted every conceivable rationale for ongoing discrimination with raw logic. Like us, they saw ending marriage discrimination as recognizing that gay people are part of our society. The Court declared that our time had come, that gay people are now part of 'we the people.'"

Alison Coleman was at home in Boston with her partner of thirteen years, Lisa Bossley, when she learned of the decision. Like everyone, she had expected the decision during the summer. "When it didn't happen I just went on with my life. Then suddenly we came home from work one day and there it was, marriage was a possibility. We both happened to be watching the news when the story came out that the Supreme Judicial Court had approved it. I just felt euphoric. I never really expected it or expected to get married—and felt like my heart was elevated. It was like being let into something that you never really wanted, or didn't realize how much you wanted, this kind of public acknowledgment of who you are, and your important relationship. We were sitting there watching TV over the counter, and I said to Lisa, so do you want to get married? And she said sure!"

FIVE

The Present as History

*A*LISON AND LISA weren't the only couple to decide to get married. The first half of 2004 saw the floodgates open in one town after another as city halls began issuing marriage licenses. Most gay people were as surprised as everyone else by the magnitude of the response. On February 12, as a fierce debate raged in the Massachusetts statehouse over the court's decision, San Francisco Mayor Gavin Newsom announced that his city would start issuing marriage licenses to same-sex couples. Hundreds turned out the next day. Over the next 28 days, the nation was treated to the spectacle of more than 4,000 gay and lesbian couples lining up to claim their licenses.[1] Straight supporters showed up with roses and champagne; passing cars honked their horns in support. *Newsweek* commented on how "ordinary" looking the people were who crowded city hall: "Mothers pushing strollers stood behind dads with infants strapped to their chests; seniors mingled with businessmen; elderly parents struggled with their corsages and brothers-in-law fiddled with their video cameras, while children slid across shiny marble in their dress clothes."[2]

Other municipalities soon followed San Francisco's lead. A

clerk in Sandoval County, New Mexico, near Albuquerque, began giving out licenses on February 20; word spread rapidly, and sixty-two couples got them that day before the state attorney general insisted that the clerk stop. A week later, Mayor Jason West of New Paltz, New York, performed twenty-five marriages in his Hudson River Valley village before being stopped. Multnomah County, Oregon, which includes Portland, began issuing licenses on March 3. By the time a county circuit judge ordered the county to stop seven weeks later, more than 3,000 couples had gotten licenses in Oregon. Everywhere the story was the same: an official's announcement that they would issue licenses produced an outpouring of enthusiasm.

The same jubilation greeted the arrival of marriage in Massachusetts on Monday, May 17. No one knew until the last minute if the court's ruling would go into effect, since Governor Mitt Romney and right-wing legal groups fought it to the end. But when it became clear that marriage would finally become legal for same-sex couples on the 17th, the city of Cambridge staked its claim to be the first Massachusetts municipality to issue marriage licenses by announcing it would begin a minute after midnight. The line started forming twenty-four hours earlier, when two women in their fifties, Marcia Hams and Susan Shepherd, walked up the city hall steps at midnight to claim first place. They had met when they both were machinists at General Electric and had been together for twenty-seven years. By midnight the next night, more than 250 couples had joined them in line and a crowd of ten thousand had gathered to cheer them on.

What Marriage Meant

Why did getting married matter so much to so many people in a culture that seemed no longer to place much stock in the institution?

Many people waiting in line that night in Cambridge and the next morning in Boston pointed to the problems they and their partners had faced in their dealings with hospitals, loan offices, schools, and employers. After eighteen years together, Peter and John were annoyed that they still couldn't get family insurance. They worried about what would happen to the house they'd bought together when one of them died. And they remembered how when Peter's grandmother passed away, John couldn't attend the entire funeral with him. "John's been part of my family," Peter recalled. "Both our families are very close, and he was the only one that couldn't take bereavement leave off of work to be there. All my sisters, their husbands, they got to be there. He had to miss the morning part of the funeral, couldn't come for the wake, couldn't come until later." Everyone wondered why he couldn't be there. So did they. "You know," he said, "these injustices come up."

Kate had also been with her partner for eighteen years. There had been times when one of them was working and the other was in school and they'd sit down at tax time and calculate "what taxes we would have paid, had we been married. Then we figured out what taxes we paid separately, and we called it the lesbian tax. Every year it was like, hmm, was it worth $3,000 to be lesbians this year?" They always agreed "it was worth it, but we've both been very aware of the financial impact" of the fact that they couldn't get married.

Two women who'd been together for nineteen years told of the time one of them went into the hospital for breast surgery and her partner "wasn't allowed in there." They "had to fight, and fight," and "I ended up signing myself out." Another woman had tried to renegotiate her partner's student loans with an agency. "I get on the phone and talk to these people, and they say, well, who are you? And I say, I'm her partner. And they go, so what." So she "had to send in a form that says it's okay for me to talk for her," a different form for each loan. "This is insane," she thought.

In San Francisco, Portland, and Boston alike, significantly more women than men got marriage licenses. In Massachusetts, two-thirds of the 752 couples to get marriage licenses on the first day were lesbian, and 40 percent of those couples had children living with them.[3] This shouldn't be surprising, since having children raised the stakes for everyone. When their kids were born they had taken care of all the paperwork—the wills and health proxies and trusts—many of them had never bothered with before. But "while that's there, you never really know that those legal documents would uphold in a court of law," one mother commented. And she wondered about all the gay parents who didn't have the money or time to get those documents prepared. What would happen to them "when there's some sort of tragedy?" Another woman remembered that when she got a job with health insurance she couldn't put her partner's children on it, even though they had raised the children together for years.

But the people waiting in line didn't just want the rights,

protections, and benefits that married couples had. They wanted to be recognized as fully equal to them. The fierce resistance to same-sex marriage had impressed on people the power of marriage to symbolize that equality. Especially in San Francisco, waiting in line to get a license came to feel like an act of civil disobedience as numerous government officials and right-wing legal groups raced to shut the line down. But even in Massachusetts, no one could forget how hard Governor Romney, the Catholic Church, and many legislators had fought to keep them from getting there.

"This isn't just benefits, and it isn't just the legal issue," Robert insisted as he waited outside Boston City Hall. He regarded the freedom to marry as a sign of his full equality and humanity. "I woke up a couple of days ago," he remembered, "and said to myself, oh my God, we're going to be equal to other human beings." Deb said she "was sitting on the subway this morning coming in here, and I'm looking around, thinking, okay, I'll be just like them. . . . We're no longer second-class citizens. That's what it really means."

The sudden possibility of getting married made many people wonder if they had been complicit before with their second-class citizenship. They had accepted and taken for granted that they would never have the rights and protections of marriage, and now wondered why. Domestic partnership and civil unions, which had once seemed like a huge advance, even preferable to some as an alternative to marriage, now seemed unacceptably "separate and unequal," as people took to saying. Why had they put up with it? "There's so many ways in which we know we have had second-class citizenship because of our lack of access to this civil institution," one woman mused.

Some people in line said they had always wanted to get married, even though they never expected it would actually be possible. Others had never thought of doing it at all—until they suddenly could. "When you knew that you couldn't do it, you didn't think about it, because it was sort of painful," Anne commented. "So I don't think I realized how much I wanted to do it, until I could do it. My parents have been married for forty years, my sister's been married for fourteen years, it's something we do in our family. So once it was real, I realized it was something I really wanted to do."

The rush to marry bore testimony to the continuing power of marriage as a symbol of personal commitment and as a means of gaining recognition for that commitment from others. "First and foremost, I love this woman and she loves me," one woman said to explain why she was in line, and marriage was "the best sign of a commitment that you can make." Another woman commented on how many of the "younger people" at her job had gotten married. "It's a long process of their planning it, and sharing that with people, and being excited, and doing it with their families." She'd been with her partner for more than twenty-five years, and now that she was planning her own wedding she was struck by how much it meant to her to "be able to talk about that with people, and have people involved in that." She noticed even more than before the "power of marriage as a social institution that gives people credibility within the community."

Still, not everyone raced to get married. For many couples, the fact that it suddenly was an option—that they suddenly *could* and *had* to make a choice about getting married—led to soul-searching about the meaning of marriage for their relationship as well as thoughtful debate about what securing this right might mean for the larger movement for social justice.

Some people who decided to get married, especially feminists, continued to be critical of how marriage allocated benefits and served to elevate some relationships over others. "We're progressive people who have really thought a lot about what the pros and cons are of this, which is something that I don't think a lot of heterosexuals think about," Karen commented. Getting married was "not going to have a big impact in our lives personally, quite honestly, because we're deeply committed to each other, we're deeply loyal to our friends and our family and each other." But she, too, thought it was important to be there, because so long as marriage rights were denied, "the inequalities can only ferment and seep through our system of justice," and "equality can't happen." Another woman agreed that she had "mixed feelings" about marriage. "But then, like everybody, when it happened, it just felt like a door opened, and it's momentous and historic and important. I've had my commitment ceremony, so I'm not doing this for the sanction of the state, but because it has made it clearer that this is about second-class citizenship."

Shortly after she got married, Evelynn Hammond wrote some friends about her complex reactions to the experience:

As I walked to my office I thought—nothing will ever be the same and yet picking up the license was the same experience anyone straight would have had. I wish I had adequate words to describe all the events of last week—but I don't yet. My feelings aren't really about the personal aspects of same-sex marriage. I don't feel any differently about Alexandra or my commitment to her than I did before last week. It is the historic aspect of this that feels strange, pleasant, and disquieting. I keep ruminating on what it means to be "normal" versus "not normal"; "different" and "not-different." I feel like I was a part of the dismantling of the Berlin Wall—the dismantling of something that was literally both concrete and ideological.

What Is Defended by the "Defense of Marriage Act"?

The images of joyous lesbian and gay couples and their kids that filled America's television sets in the winter of 2004 produced widely varying responses. Their ordinary humanity and devotion to one another touched many Americans. But their audacity in claiming the right to marry horrified many others, especially religious conservatives. On February 24, just two weeks after Mayor Newsom had thrown open the doors of City Hall, President Bush himself called for a constitutional amendment that would shut those doors forever.

Why did marriage galvanize such strident opposition, as well as such excitement? For all the ferocity of the debate unleashed by the developments in San Francisco and Boston, the debate over marriage was only the latest stage in a long-running debate over gay equality. The fiercest opponents of same-sex marriage had pushed the Defense of Marriage Act through Congress eight years earlier and had been fighting gay rights for more than a generation. Long before proposing a constitutional amendment to ban same-sex marriage, they had opposed gay rights ordinances, the right of gay couples to adopt children, and the appearance of gay characters in the media. For more than twenty years they had led referendum campaigns against gay rights ordinances. In 1996, the Southern Baptist Convention had called for a boycott of Disney because Disneyland hosted gay theme nights and the company had established a domestic partnership program that "accepts and embraces homosexual relationships for the purpose of insurance benefits." In 2001, Focus on the Family had opposed the decision of New York Governor George Pataki to make benefits available to the gay partners as well as the spouses of victims of the September 11 terrorist attacks.[4] Many of the arguments they made against same-sex marriage—that it would harm children and undermine the sanctity of marriage, the nation's morality, and very idea of gender difference— echoed the arguments they had once made against gay rights measures that now enjoyed wide popular support.

Still, "defending marriage" as the union of one man and one woman had special symbolic significance for the opponents of gay rights. Many of its opponents saw "gay marriage" as both the ultimate sign of gay equality and the final blow to their traditional ideal of marriage, which had been buffeted by thirty years of change. Their arguments reflected this, and even as they recapitulated old themes, they registered the profound change that had taken place in American attitudes toward gay people.

The link between the "defense of marriage" and opposition to gender equality was especially noteworthy. The association of homosexuality with gender inversion and role reversal has shaped public attitudes toward both gay people and gender conventions throughout the twentieth century. At times that association has produced a compelling mixture of fascination and awe, which was palpable among the thousands of heterosexuals who flocked to see the female and male impersonators at Harlem's drag balls in the 1920s and 1930s, and among the millions who danced to the disco beat of Sylvester and Ru-Paul half a century later. But at times of dramatic change in gender roles, opponents of change have often used that association to attack those changes and to stigmatize gay people. This could be seen in the early twentieth century, when many doctors condemned women's quest for equality as a sign of degeneration. And it could be seen in the simultaneous enactment of laws restricting women's employment and gay people's visibility in response to the crisis in the male-dominated family caused by the Great Depression of the 1930s. Over the course of the twentieth century, advances and reversals in the rights of lesbians and gay men have almost always been linked to similar changes in the status of women.

After the rise of the women's movement and gay movement in the 1960s and 1970s, the opponents of both linked them as much as many of their participants did. The specter of "homosexual marriage" was part of what doomed the battle to ratify the Equal Rights Amendment. The Amendment easily passed both houses of Congress in 1972 and was ratified by thirty of the necessary thirty-eight states within a year. But in the next two years, conservatives brought that momentum to a halt. Some of their most effective arguments warned that the ERA would not just end sex discrimination but would also challenge the very notion of difference between men and women by rendering unconstitutional the legal recognition of such differences. Three claims about how the ERA would subvert everyday common sense about gender differences were especially evocative: it would require unisex toilets, the drafting of women into the military, and the recognition of "homosexual marriage."[5] ERA supporters rejected those arguments but could not overcome them. Indeed, the effectiveness of these arguments against the ERA is probably one reason few gay activists imagined that marriage rights were possible to pursue in the 1970s.

Beginning in the 1970s, the growing Christian Right linked changes in women's roles to the growing freedom of gay people in more powerful and enduring ways. A fundamentalist revival characterized the 1960s and 1970s as much as the sexual revolution did. In 1979, leaders of several "superchurches" at the forefront of that revival organized the Moral Majority to counteract what they saw as the nation's slide into immorality. Drawing on a strong base in independent fundamentalist churches and the power of evangelical television shows and networks to communicate their message, the movement rapidly grew. The Traditional Values Coalition, Focus on the Family, Christian Coalition, and other groups formed in its wake shared its central belief that restoring the Christian family was the key to restoring the nation's moral order.[6]

In his 1980 book *Listen, America!*, Jerry Falwell, the founder of the Moral Majority, warned that changes in gender roles and the growth of the gay movement were two sides of the same coin: "We would not be having the present moral crisis regarding the homosexual movement if men and women accepted their proper roles as designated by God," he contended. "In the Christian home the father is responsible to exercise spiritual control and to be the head over his wife and children; 'for the husband is the head of the wife, even as Christ is the head of the church' (Ephesians 5:23). . . . In the Christian home the woman is to be submissive; 'wives, submit yourselves unto your own husbands, as unto the Lord' (Ephesians 5:22). Homosexuality is Satan's diabolical attack upon the family, God's order in Creation."[7] The link was so obvious to Falwell that he didn't need to explain it.

Stated in these stark terms, such arguments were unlikely to persuade a majority of Americans by the beginning of the twenty-first century, but they found a powerful constituency in the movement for "traditional family values." That movement's concern that, as Rev. Falwell put it, "feminists desire to eliminate God-given differences that exist between the sexes"[8] helped inspire its fervent opposition to granting marriage rights to gay couples. Glenn Stanton of Focus on the Family warned in 2003 that "homosexual marriage" would mean "the terms 'husband' and 'wife' would become merely words with no meaning. . . . Gender would become nothing."[9] The movement's "defense of marriage" as something available only to a man and woman was premised on the belief that God had ordained certain roles in marriage exclusively to men as "husbands" and women as "wives." The movement's opposition to "homosexual marriage" was inspired in good part by its fear that allowing two people of the same sex to marry would ratify the transformation of marriage over the last thirty years into an institution of legal equality and gender neutrality, in which most people expect and are expected to negotiate the terms of their own relationships free of legally mandated gender roles.

Such concerns stood behind many of the arguments made against gay marriage. Since most Americans were unprepared to accept fundamentalist prescriptions for wifely behavior, anti-marriage activists typically sought to frame their arguments in ways that would appeal to what seemed commonsense ideas about marriage's purpose. In the debate over DOMA (Defense of Marriage Act) and the federal constitutional amendment, religious leaders and quite a few congressmen cited scripture to argue that the purpose of marriage was procreation. This had a certain "common-sense" ring to it, even though neither the capacity nor the intention to procreate had ever been a requirement of marriage. GLAD conclusively demonstrated this in the Massachusetts case, and adoption as well as the new reproductive technologies had given every couple, gay or straight, fertile or infertile, the capacity to bring children into their lives. But when religious conservatives referred to "procreation," they often used it as shorthand for a larger set of assumptions about the roles of husbands and wives, including women's need to accept that their primary duty in life is to be mothers.

The right wing's most resonant arguments opposed gay couples' marriage rights under the guise of defending the interests of children. "Unisex marriages," as some foes took to calling them, simply did not create a good environment for raising children, they claimed, despite all of the evidence to the contrary.

Such arguments built on a long tradition of antigay rhetoric, but also diverged from it in ways that revealed just how far the country had moved on gay issues. A decade before arguments about the fitness of gay couples as parents moved to the center of the marriage debate, they got an extensive airing as growing numbers of couples sought joint adoption of children. Along with the growing acceptance of gay people, the research studies showing no ill effects on children seem to have influenced public opinion as well as the courts. In 1977, only 14 percent of Americans thought gay people should be allowed to adopt children. That number doubled to 29 percent by 1992, and it jumped to almost 50 percent just eight years later, in one more sign of the dramatic change in attitudes in the 1990s.[10]

Fears about whether or not the children of gay couples would turn out alright often indirectly expressed fears about whether or not those children would become homosexual themselves, notwithstanding a generation of research showing that was not the case. But these fears also expressed the lingering anxiety of some heterosexuals that the legitimization or normalization of homosexuality would have an effect on their own children as well, causing their children to become gay. For decades, many of the most strident opponents of gay rights had been inspired by such fears and made them central to their depiction of the "homosexual threat."

Public authorities and hate groups alike have often stigmatized social outsiders—be they Jews or gypsies or homosexuals—as child stealers or child molesters, because concern about children links people's broadest fears about the reproduction of the familiar social order to their deepest and most intimate fears about the safety of their own children—and about whether their children will reproduce their way of life, be it their religion, race, or sexuality. In her 1977 campaign against Miami's gay rights ordinance, Anita Bryant brilliantly mobilized that demonic image of homosexuals through news-paper ads and the very name of her organization, "Save Our Children." In the antigay hate literature that flooded states and municipalities during the referendum campaigns of the late 1980s and 1990s, homosexuals were often depicted in this way. Christian Right organizations distributed thousands of copies of "The Gay Agenda," a video that effectively juxta-posed discussions of pedophilia with images of gay teachers and gay parents marching with their children in Gay Pride parades, which made it easy for viewers to imagine they were molesters showing off their prey.

Those demonic stereotypes became less effective when peo-ple became more familiar with gay people, as their friends and relatives came out to them and they saw gay people treated in more humane and respectful ways in the media. In 1977, two-thirds of Americans objected to lesbians or gay men being hired as elementary school teachers, the last place a child mo-lester should be (two-thirds expressed no concern about gay salespersons). Fifteen years later, in 1992, half still rejected the idea of their child having a gay elementary school teacher. A decade later, about 60 percent were willing to see gay elemen-tary school teachers, and two-thirds found gay high school teachers acceptable. The experience of knowing someone gay had an enormous impact on people's opinions. A 1993 survey found that two-thirds of the respondents who had a close gay friend or family member would not worry if their child's teacher were gay or lesbian; only a third of those without a close gay friend or relative said the same thing.[11]

But such concerns continue to animate the fiercest opposi-tion to gay rights. Indeed, much of the debate over same-sex marriage and gay rights more generally hinges on the cultural divide in American society between modernist and fundamentalist views of human nature. Many scholars now argue that the ancient belief that homosexuality was a form of sinful behavior in which anyone might engage was superceded in the late nineteenth century by the modernist understanding that the homosexual is a distinct category of person. As Michel Foucault famously described this evolution, "the sodomite had been a temporary aberration; the homosexual was now a species."[12] But many Americans never accepted this new understanding of sexuality.

By and large, Americans who support gay rights tend to believe sexual identity is a stable, intrinsic, and enduring condition over which people have no control, whereas those who disapprove of homosexuality are much more likely to believe it is a choice, and a sinful one at that. A major Pew Foundation study conducted in early 2004 found that a person's belief or disbelief in the mutability of homosexual identity was a more powerful predictor of their attitudes toward gay people than education, knowing someone gay, or "general ideological beliefs." Two-thirds of those who believed someone could change their homosexuality had an unfavorable view of gay people, whereas 60 percent of those who believed that being gay was an immutable condition over which people had no choice were favorably disposed.[13]

By the winter of 2003–2004, when the marriage issue briefly dominated American political debate, the country was evenly divided on this question. Two out of five Americans thought homosexuality was something people were born with or was fixed so early in life they had no control over it. But an equal number, another two out of five, believed it was simply a choice or preference, which people could change. Half of Americans with an opinion on the matter, in other words, simply do not believe homosexuals are a discrete minority of people. One of President Bush's first public statements on the marriage debate in July 2003 suggests the prevalence of such views. In a tortured comment in which he sought to appear tolerant while also appealing to his backers on the Christian Right, he cautioned Americans that homosexuals shouldn't be singled out, since, as he put it, "we're all sinners."[14]

The belief that homosexuality is a sinful choice instead of a minority status is especially pronounced among people with a fundamentalist or evangelical worldview. Fundamentalist Protestants are more than twice as likely to believe that someone can change their sexual orientation than either mainline Protestants or Catholics (65 percent compared to 26 and 30 percent, respectively). Indeed, almost three-quarters of evangelicals who are deeply involved in their churches and religious life believe that homosexuals can change, and 93 percent of them believe homosexuality is an immoral choice.

As a result, evangelicals are more likely to fear that any government, religious, or media legitimization of homosexuality threatens the stability of heterosexuality itself by making homosexuality seem a more acceptable, even appealing choice. They worry especially about youth being exposed to such temptation, so take great care to prevent their children from having any exposure to gay people. More than two-thirds of Catholics would permit their children to play in the home of a friend who has a gay parent; but only a fifth of evangelicals would. Almost 60 percent of Catholics would hire a gay babysitter, but only 10 percent of Protestant fundamentalists would. Fundamentalists are twice as likely as most Americans to keep books with gay characters away from their children.

During the 1996 debate over the Employment Non-Discrimination Act, which would have banned antigay discrimination in hiring, some of its opponents evoked its potential consequences for young people to explain their opposition. Senator John Ashcroft, for one, opposed the bill because engaging "in a homosexual lifestyle . . . is a choice which can be made and unmade," and ending discrimination in employment might result in boys coming into contact with gay men who would influence them to make a bad choice. "I am worried about youngsters in our society," he argued. "I think there are times when young men are unsure about themselves when they are in transition, when they have identified perhaps more with their mothers than with their fathers, and they move from boyhood to manhood. Those are critical times when role models are very important. I think Senator Nickles was on target when he said that we have to be careful of who we have in the Boy Scouts."[15]

Most gay people found it difficult to believe that anyone could think their sexual orientation was a choice or that granting equal rights to gay people would influence children to become gay. Many could tell stories about how they had discovered and then resisted their own sexual orientation, given the social pressures against being gay. Being raised by heterosexuals hadn't turned them into heterosexuals, so why should the reverse be true? Then many came to resent the implication of the question itself, since gay life did no harm and for them was a positive good, and even if some people could change their sexual orientation (like their religion), it would not justify discrimination against gay people.

But the question of choice became an increasingly important element of the national debate over gay equality in the 1990s. A steady barrage of stories in the media about research studies showing that homosexuality was genetically or biologically determined was countered by an equally steady campaign by antigay activists to insist that homosexuals could change—that, in effect, homosexuals could be converted to heterosexuality just as Jews or Muslims could be converted to Christianity. Most famously, in the late 1990s Christian Right leaders began publicizing "reparative therapy" programs that they claimed could "convert" homosexuals into heterosexuals. The focus of these programs on "saving" individual souls from homosexuality allowed the Right to moderate its image when its outright demonization of homosexuals became less plausible and acceptable to most Americans.[16] The programs drew on psychological theories that had long been discredited by the American Psychological Association and were condemned by most mainline Protestant and Catholic leaders, and the "ex-gay" movement was regularly embarassed by "ex-ex-gays" who deserted and denounced it as a sham. But the Christian Right's new focus on the claim that homosexuality was a choice reinforced old stereotypes about homosexual seduction and provided the right with a subtle but powerful argument to use against any arrangement—from domestic partnership to marriage—that might seem to give social support to a sinfully choosen "lifestyle."

Civil Rights and Segregationist Theology

No historical study can resolve the complex debate over marriage, but a historical perspective may help illuminate it. I've already shown how deeply the gay movement was influenced by the black civil rights movement. I want to conclude by commenting on how that movement's experience in the 1950s and 1960s might help us to understand what is at stake in the national debate over gay couples' right to marry and the role played in that debate by religion. The civil rights movement confronted the deeply intertwined issues of faith and marriage long before the gay movement did, and there are lessons we can draw from the parallels in their experiences.[17]

Most people imagine that the black and gay movements have had utterly different relationships to organized religion. We all know how divided our churches are today over the issue of homosexuality. But the well-known civil rights leadership of Dr. Martin Luther King and other clergymen leads most people to imagine that the churches were always united in support of civil rights, a historical perception reinforced by today's religious conservatives who try to make their opposition to gay rights seem more mainstream by claiming that they have always recognized the morality and legitimacy of *black*—as opposed to *homosexual*—civil rights. But in fact, American Christians once were as deeply divided over the issue of race as they are today over the issue of homosexuality. The Presbyterian, Methodist, and Baptist denominations split over the issue of slavery during the Civil War era. It took the Presbyterians more than a century to reunite. The Baptists never did.

In the century following Emancipation (as in the century before it), many Southern white Christians viewed the segregation of the races and the prohibition against miscegenation as part of God's plan for humankind. A pamphlet published at the height of the post–Civil War struggles over the meaning of emancipation warned that "a man can not commit so great an offense against his race, against his country, against his God, in any other way, as to give his daughter in marriage to a negro—a beast—or to take one their females for his wife. . . . The states or people that favor this equality and amalgamation of the white and black races, God will exterminate."[18]

In the 1950s and 1960s, many whites continued to buttress their defense of segregation with what some historians have referred to as "segregationist theology."[19] A lower court judge ruled in the *Loving* interracial marriage case in the mid-1960s, for example, "Almighty God created the races white, black, yellow, malay, and red, and he placed them on separate continents. And but for the interference with his arrangement there would be no cause for such marriages. The fact that he separated the races shows that he did not intend for the races to mix." He based this claim on the widely accepted segregationist interpretation of Paul's assertion in Acts 17:26 that God "decreed how long each nation should flourish and what the boundaries of its territory should be." In 1955 the Florida Supreme Court had upheld segregation using a similar biblical rationale in a ruling that explained "When God created man, He allotted each race to his continent according to color."[20]

The judges' proclamations were echoed from the pulpits of the region's white churches. A young Southern pastor named

Jerry Falwell, for one, preached that segregation was part of God's plan. Falwell declared in 1958 that "If the Supreme Court had known God's word, I am quite confident that the 1954 school desegregation decision would never have been made." He went on to dismiss the advocates of desegregation as the agents of Moscow and "the devil." And just as Falwell and the rest of the Religious Right have recently tried to make gay marriage rights the specter haunting every debate about gay rights, so he and other conservative white clergy fifty years ago held up interracial marriage as the logical, inevitable, and most horrifying result of any move toward desegregation. In that 1958 sermon, Rev. Falwell warned that integration would ultimately "destroy our race. If we mix the races in schools, in churches, the ultimate end will be the social mixing which can only lead to marital relationships."[21]

Almost forty years later, the by-then prominent founder of the Moral Majority and crusader against gay rights inadvertently confirmed the ubiquity of such segregationist thought in Southern white churches when he was asked to comment on his now discarded and discredited opinion. At the time of the sermon, he explained, he was simply a young, inexperienced pastor following "the party line and the denominational line." It was only later, he said, that he was prepared to "buck the tide . . . [and] go against public opinion" on the race issue. Although Rev. Falwell was understandably trying to rehabilitate his moral credibility, his explanation confirmed that the *tide of public opinion* in the Southern white churches *ran against* desegregation and interracial marriage. The gay movement is not the first civil rights movement to face determined religious opposition.

Many of the biblical stories cited today to show that homosexuality is a form of sinful behavior that violates God's will for male and female were used by segregationists to different ends. Some antigay churchmen have found antigay significance in the fact that God created Adam and Eve—"not Adam and Steve," as Jesse Helms quoted a black minister as saying during the Defense of Marriage Act debate—and commanded them to "be fruitful and multiply." But some segregationists found a different meaning in the story. According to Charles Carroll's *The Tempter of Eve*, a widely influential racist diatribe in the early twentieth-century South, Eve's tempter was not a snake but a black man, and their race-mixing was the first sin.[22] During the debate over DOMA, Senator Robert Byrd cited the story of Noah to remind his colleagues that God intended couples (one male and one female) to "be fruitful and multiply, and replenish the earth." But fifty years earlier, some segregationists found a different lesson in the story of Noah: that in Noah's time there had been so much race-mixing that "God destroyed 'all flesh' in that part of the world for that one sin," as one 1954 pamphleteer declared. "Only Noah was 'perfect in his generation' . . . so God saved him and his family to rebuild the Adamic Race."[23] As the historian Jane Dailey observes in her careful study of this theological tradition, "Again and again God's wrath is aroused by the sin of miscegenation, and the people feel the awful weight of his punishment." Many white Southern Christians believed that Sodom and Gomorrah had been "destroyed for this sin," the sin of miscegenation, "as was the Tower of Babel, where, in a failed effort to protect racial purity, God dispersed the peoples across the globe." As Dailey concludes, "In this tradition, miscegenation—or, more commonly, amalgamation or mongrelization—was the original sin, the root of all corruption in humankind."[24]

It is often forgotten today just how much white people's fears about interracial marriage were at the emotional core of their fears about integration in general, and how much such fears accounted for the virulence of the opposition to school and neighborhood desegregation in particular. But it was widely recognized at the time by blacks and whites alike. Reflecting on an incident that almost led to his getting lynched, the black writer James Weldon Johnson observed in 1933, "Through it all I discerned one clear and certain truth: in the core of the heart of the American race problem the sex factor is rooted; rooted so deeply that it is not always recognized when it shows at the surface."[25] Thirty years later, in 1964, the *Christian Century* observed that interracial marriage was "the most delicate, sensitive, emotion-charged aspect of racial discrimination."[26]

Lessons from the Past

As should be clear by now, I do not mean to draw facile comparisons between the historical experiences of African-Americans and lesbians and gay men (or to ignore the existence of people who share both experiences). One sign of the historical difference between their experiences is that securing marriage rights looms larger in the quest for gay equality today than it did for the civil rights movement in the 1950s, when black Southerners focused instead on their systematic exclusion from the franchise, educational opportunities, decent-paying jobs, and most parks, hotels, and restrooms. More evidence of the difference is provided by the fact that between the late nineteenth century and the 1950s, hundreds of black men who violated or were suspected of violating the ban on marriage or sex with white women paid a penalty of death at the hands of lynch mobs. Claiming the two experiences have been the same does no justice to history and no service to the gay cause.

Nonetheless, there are at least four important lessons we can learn from the history of the black civil rights struggle and the opposition to interracial marriage that help us better understand the opposition to gay equality and marriage rights.

First, this history helps clarify what is at stake in the debate over marriage, and why it incites such passion. The very severity with which whites policed the ban on interracial marriage reminds us how deeply they regarded the freedom to marry as an emblem of the citizenship and equality they would deny to African-Americans. Marriage bans play an integral role in reinforcing broader patterns of inequality. As Gunnar Myrdal observed in his classic 1944 sociological study of Southern race relations, *An American Dilemma*, "what white people really want is to keep the Negroes in a lower status. 'Intermarriage' itself is resented because it would be a supreme indication of 'social equality.'"[27] White Southerners also opposed interracial marriage so forcefully because they feared it would dissolve the very boundaries between black and white—the very fiction of "the purity of the white race"—that were the foundation of white supremacy.

Today, many conservatives unapologetically argue that they oppose granting marriage rights to gay people because they would be a sign of *gay* equality and would undermine the strict boundaries between sexual "normality" and "abnormality." In the 1996 debate over the Defense of Marriage Act, Representative Charles Canady of Florida was very explicit that "what is really at stake" in DOMA was "whether the law of this country should treat homosexual relationships as morally equivalent to heterosexual relationships." Rep. Lamar Smith of Texas warned that allowing gay couples to marry would "legitimize unnatural and immoral behavior" and accede to gay people's desire for "full social acceptance."[28]

Second, this history may help illuminate the vexed question of the relationship between civil rights and gay rights. Today some religious conservatives, both black and white, contend that there can be no equation between the civil rights due a racial minority and the rights claimed by people whose sinful choices violate religious principle. But this perspective on civil rights does not come to terms with the depth and power of racist ideology in the 1950s. While black activists claimed they were seeking the civil rights due a minority, white supremacists did not accept that perspective on the conflict anymore than antigay clergy do today. Segregationists fought the civil rights movement not just with laws and police dogs but with an entire cosmology that made the separation of the races a commandment of God. Many Southern white Christians believed integration and interracial marriage were against God's word with at least as much moral fervor and sincere conviction as today inspire some Christians' opposition to gay rights and gay marriage.

Indeed, the Southern struggle over civil rights does more than just remind us that humans have often called on the infallible and timeless authority of God to support moral postures that later generations regard as all too fallible and shaped by particular historical circumstances. It also reminds us that segregationists were as preoccupied with sinful behavior and choices as the opponents of gay rights are today. White supremacists regarded blacks as inferior, to be sure, just as some antigay activists today regard homosexuals as degenerate. But we should never forget how often the demonization of subordinate groups as sexually aberrant and dangerous has served to justify their subordination. Homosexuals are not the first group to be demonized as sexual sinners and predators. The most pernicious and enduring example of this in American history is provided by the defenders of white supremacy, who for generations justified segregation and lynching alike by alleging that African-Americans had voracious sexual appetites that threatened white women and racial purity.

Attributing immoral or abnormal sexual practices exclusively to subordinate groups and outsiders has allowed dominant groups to set themselves apart from their subordinates, to assert their own purity, and to police their own ranks against any behavior that might undermine their separate and privileged status. The opponents of gay rights often argue that homosexuality is a choice, not a stable status like race. But in the 1950s the boundaries between black and white did not seem so stable. In fact, it was their all-too-apparent instability and permeability that helped account for the fierce opposition to integration and interracial marriage. No matter how much whites demonized black men as sexual predators, their real fear was that allowing black and white youth to socialize under conditions of equality in integrated schools or neighborhoods might lead to a white daughter's sinful choice to marry or have sex with a black man, which would result in a family losing its racial status in a single generation. Recall what Jerry Falwell warned in 1958: "If we mix the races in schools, in churches, the ultimate end will be the social mixing which can only lead to marital relationships."

The third lesson of this history is cautionary: that both the advocates and opponents of same-sex marriage have exaggerated its likely effects. The segregationists were wrong, after all. The legalization of interracial marriage did *not* end notions of racial difference or patterns of racial domination and inequality, though it surely has complicated them. Similarly, it seems clear that the fears of those opposing same-sex marriage that it will undermine heterosexuality and gender difference are as exaggerated as the hopes of some marriage advocates that it alone will secure full gay and gender equality.

Still, a fourth lesson is that people and ideas change. Racism has not disappeared, but the theology of Dr. King has triumphed over segregationist theology so decisively that his religious opponents have been almost entirely forgotten. The fact that even conservative religious thought about black civil rights and interracial marriage has changed so fundamentally in the last generation suggests that today's religious opposition to gay rights and same-sex marriage may be less intransigent than it seems.

The Christian Right's fierce opposition to gay rights is already a minority position among Protestant denominations, most of which have supported laws banning discrimination in employment and other spheres of secular life for more than a generation. Many of those mainline denominations still prohibit the recognition of gay marriages or the leadership of openly gay people in the church itself. But even here change seems likely. From my perspective as a historian, the most significant aspect of the Episcopal Church's wrenching debate in 2003 over the ordination as bishop of an openly gay man, V. Gene Robinson, is that it took place at all. It will never again be possible for conservative religious leaders to claim that every Christian shares their views on the place of lesbians and gay men in religious life, or that people of faith must regard homosexual conduct as a sin. The Episcopalian controversy drew unprecedented attention to the debate that has been intensifying for thirty years in every major faith in this country, and to the fact that many devout Christians, Jews, and Muslims fully accept gay people as part of God's plan for humankind. Theirs is still a minority religious position, but *suddenly* and *irreversibly*, it is an *imaginable* position.

The Present as History

Marriage is only the latest chapter in a long debate over gay equality, not the first, and certainly not the last. But the history of marriage has given this debate special significance for all sides because the freedom to marry, including the right to choose one's partner in marriage, has come to be regarded as a fundamental civil right and a powerful symbol of full equality and citizenship. Many fundamentalists now strongly oppose the right of gay couples to marry because they see that right as the ultimate symbol of the equality they would deny to gay people—and because they fear it would ratify the growing freedom of heterosexual men and women to negotiate the terms of their marital relationships without being bound by the rules that once strictly governed the roles of "husbands" and "wives." Many lesbians and gay men have embraced the campaign for marriage rights because they, too, see marriage equality as a fundamental sign of their equality and full citizenship, and because securing the many rights, benefits, protections, and obligations conveyed by marriage would have so many palpable effects on their lives.

No one can predict the future of the debate over gay marriage or the place of gay people in American society. That said, it is hard to think of another group whose circumstances and public reputation have changed so decisively in so little time. For several decades now, and especially since the 1990s, Americans have become more familiar with their lesbian and gay neighbors and more supportive of them. Above all, there has been a sea change in the attitudes of the young, who have grown up in a world where they know gay people and see them treated with the respect any human deserves.

The opponents of gay equality recognize these changes too. Their campaign to pass a constitutional amendment on marriage stems from their determination to impose the bigotry and inequality of the past on the generations of the future by writing them into the fundamental law of the land. The tide of history is running against them. But nothing in history is inevitable. As always, our future lies in our own hands.

Acknowledgments

*A*s someone accustomed to writing very long books that take a very long time to complete (one down, another almost done), writing a short book like this in three months has been an unexpected challenge. My first thanks go to my publisher, Liz Maguire, for persuading me to write the book and then making sure I got it done.

This is a short book without elaborate footnotes (for those, see *Gay New York*), but it relies on an immense body of historical scholarship on postwar American culture, the civil rights movement, the gay movement and AIDS, and marriage. I would like to note my special indebtedness to the work of Nancy Cott, John D'Emilio, Peggy Pascoe, and David Chambers, and to the historians' amicus brief submitted in the Massachusetts case of *Goodridge v. Department of Public Health*. At an early stage in the book's development, I was fortunate to attend a special session on the history of marriage at the March 2004 annual meeting of the Organization of American Historians, and the superb presentations by the historians Estelle Freedman, Hendrik Hartog, and Peggy Pascoe both confirmed some of my thinking and suggested important new lines of approach.

Why Marriage? also draws heavily on the research and thinking I have done for my book *Gay New York: Gender, Urban Culture, and the*

Making of the Gay Male World, 1890–1940 (Basic Books, 1994) and my nearly completed next book, *The Strange Career of the Closet: Gay Culture, Consciousness, and Politics from the Second World War to the Gay Liberation Era* (Basic Books, forthcoming). Numerous paragraphs in Chapters 1 and 2 draw on sections I drafted for the amicus brief that a group of nine other historians and I submitted to the U.S. Supreme Court in the case of *Lawrence v. Texas*, and for their comments on those sections I am much indebted to my co-signatories, especially John D'Emilio, Estelle Freedman, and Liz Kennedy. Other paragraphs draw on a short introductory essay, "Who Is Welcome at Ellis Island? AIDS Activism and the Expanding National Community," which I wrote for the program for an American Foundation for AIDS Research benefit held on Ellis Island in June 2000. The book also incorporates arguments I have developed in a series of lectures, and I especially thank my hosts at the École Normale Supérieure, the Gill Foundation's 2003 Outgiving conference, the Universities of Pennsylvania, Maryland, North Texas, and Chicago, and the Women's Breakfast at the 2003 American Historical Association Meeting for providing those occasions. Finally, the book depends on the critical historical synthesis required by years of teaching postwar American history and the history of sexuality at the University of Chicago, and all that I've learned from working with an extraordinary group of graduate students. I especially thank the undergrads who took my lesbian, gay, bisexual, and transgender history class in the fall of 2003 for their exuberant and open-minded engagement with many of the ideas that unexpectedly ended up in this book, and for serving as a living testament to the profound changes wrought in American culture in the last generation.

For their thoughtful and extremely helpful comments on a draft of the book I am indebted to Nancy Cott, Lane Fenrich, Jacqueline Goldsby, Ron Gregg, Evelynn Hammonds, David Hansell, Michael Sherry, and Jennifer Wriggins. None of them should be held responsible for any errors or opinions they tried to correct. Christine Marra and John Thomas did a terrific job of shepherding this book through its unbelievably tight schedule and copyediting. Many thanks also to the people who talked with me while they were waiting in line to get their marriage licenses outside Cambridge City Hall on May 16 and Boston City Hall on May 17, as well as the people I spoke with on other occasions who did the same in San Francisco and Portland.

And I thank my parents. Long before I read about segregationist theology, I heard about it from my father, a courageous southern white Presbyterian minister who paid dearly in the 1950s and 1960s for refusing to accept it and working for racial justice instead.

It would not have been possible to write this book so quickly without the phenomenal research assistance provided by Mike Czaplicki. Andrew Layne Martin also performed yeoman service, and Carl Nash provided critical help on a moment's notice. Frank Conaway and Margaret Schilt at the University of Chicago Library were helpful beyond the call of duty.

As always, I am indebted most of all to my partner Ron Gregg, who made this book possible by reading countless drafts, cooking way more than his share, and providing abundant insights, encouragement, and practical assistance. It may surprise some people who read this book to learn that even after ten devoted years together, Ron and I aren't champing at the bit to get married. Maybe it's just that as children of the seventies, we're not the marryin' kind; then again, maybe it's just because it isn't legal yet in Illinois. But what I don't expect to proclaim at a wedding anytime soon, I gladly proclaim here: Ron is the joy of my life, and I can't imagine my life without him.

Notes

Preface

1. Human Rights Campaign, "Truth or Consequences: The Effects of Constitutional Amendments on Marriage in Ohio, Michigan, Missouri and Utah," April 2005.

2. Steve Rosenthal, "Okay, We Lost Ohio, The Question Is, Why?" *Washington Post*, December 5, 2004. Rosenthal is the chief executive officer of Americans Coming Together, which ran the pro-Kerry Get-Out-The-Vote operation in Ohio.

3. Karen Tumulty, "The Folklore of Election '04: Debunking the Falsehoods Springing from this November's Contest," *Time*, November 15, 2004.

4. *The Economist*, November 11, 2004.

Chapter 1

1. This chapter is more extensively footnoted than the others, but it seemed important to provide documentation of the discriminatory measures it describes. The chapter draws heavily on sections I drafted for the Historians' Amicus Brief submitted in *Lawrence v. Texas*, and following it, I cite the recent work of historians on these issues. There is also a large and useful literature produced by lawyers and legal scholars. On the history of film censorship, see Gregory Black, *Hollywood Censored: Morality Codes, Catholics, and the Movies* (Cambridge: Cambridge University Press, 1994); Vito Russo, *The Celluloid Closet: Homo-*

sexuality in the Movies (New York: Harper and Row, 1981); and George Chauncey, *Gay New York: Gender, Urban Culture, and the Making of the Gay Male World, 1890-1940* (New York: Basic Books, 1994), 353 and n.57.

2. Kaier Curtin, *"We Can Always Call Them Bulgarians": The Emergence of Lesbians and Gay Men on the American Stage* (Boston: Alyson, 1987); Chauncey, *Gay New York*, 311–313.

3. David K. Johnson, *The Lavender Scare: The Cold War Persecution of Gays and Lesbians in the Federal Government* (Chicago: University of Chicago Press, 2004), 166 and passim; Robert D. Dean, *Imperial Brotherhood: Gender and the Making of Cold War Foreign Policy* (Amherst: University of Massachusetts Press, 2001).

4. Stacy Braukman, "'Nothing Else Matters But Sex': Cold War Narratives of Deviance and the Search for Lesbian Teachers in Florida, 1959–1963," *Feminist Studies* 27 (2001): 553, 555; See also 553–557, 573, and n.3.

5. Chauncey, *Gay New York*, 173, 337.

6. Ibid., 337.

7. See Chauncey, *Gay New York*, chapter 12, quotes on pp. 338, 344. Similar restrictions were imposed by the California Liquor Authority in the 1950s; see Nan Alamilla Boyd, *Wide Open Town: A History of Queer San Francisco* (Berkeley: University of California Press, 2003), 108–147. For similar policing in Buffalo, New York, see Elizabeth Lapovsky Kennedy and Madeline D. Davis, *Boots of Leather, Slippers of Gold: The History of a Lesbian Community* (New York: Routledge, 1993), 145–146.

8. Chauncey, *Gay New York*, 339.

9. John D'Emilio, *Sexual Politics, Sexual Communities: The Making of a Homosexual Minority, 1940–1970* (Chicago: University of Chicago Press, 1981), 182–184.

10. D'Emilio, *Sexual Politics*, 51; Chauncey, *Gay New York*, 340; Chauncey, *The Strange Career of the Closet: Gay Culture, Consciousness, and Politics from the Second World War to the Gay Liberation Era* (New York, Basic Books, forthcoming); John Gerassi, *The Boys of Boise: Furor, Vice, and Folly in an American City* (New York: Macmillan, 1966); Fred Fejes, "Murder, Perversion, and Moral Panic: The 1954 Media

Campaign Against Miami's Homosexuals and the Discourse of Civic Betterment," *Journal of the History of Sexuality* 9 (2000): 305–347.

11. On the Chicago group, see Jonathan Ned Katz, *Gay American History: Lesbians and Gay Men in the U.S.A.* (New York: Crowell, 1976), 385–389; Katz, *The Gay/Lesbian Almanac* (New York: Morrow, 1983), 554–561; on Mattachine, see D'Emilio, *Sexual Politics*, 115, 120–121.

12. See John D'Emilio and Estelle B. Freedman, *Intimate Matters: A History of Sexuality in America* (San Francisco/New York: Harper and Row, 1988), 150–156, 202–215; Chauncey, *Gay New York*, 137–141, 183–186, 197–198, 249–250; Paul Boyer, *Urban Masses and Moral Order in America, 1820–1920* (Cambridge: Harvard University Press, 1978), 191–219.

13. Chauncey, *Gay New York*, 172.

14. Chauncey, "A Gay World, Vibrant and Forgotten," *New York Times*, 26 June 1994, E17.

15. John D'Emilio, "The Homosexual Menace: The Politics of Sexuality in Cold War America," in *Passion and Power: Sexuality in History*, eds. Kathy Peiss and Christina Simmons, with Robert A. Padgug (Philadelphia: Temple University Press, 1989), 231; Chauncey, "The Postwar Sex Crime Panic," in *True Stories from the American Past*, ed. William Graebner (New York: McGraw-Hill, 1993), 160–178.

16. Estelle B. Freedman, "'Uncontrolled Desires': The Response to the Sexual Psychopath, 1920–1960," *Journal of American History* 74 (1987): 83–106; Chauncey, "Postwar Sex Crime Panic."

17. *Lawrence v. Texas*, No. 02-102 (June 26, 2003), Brief for Professors of History et al. as Amicus Curiae; Brief for American Civil Liberties Union et al. as Amicus Curiae; Brief for Cato Institute as Amicus Curiae.

18. Chauncey, *Gay New York*; on Chicago, see David K. Johnson, "The Kids of Fairytown: Gay Male Culture on Chicago's Near North Side in the 1930s," in Brett Beemyn, ed., *Creating a Place for Ourselves: Lesbian, Gay, and Bisexual Community Histories* (New York: Routledge, 1997), 97–118, and Chad Heap, "Slumming: The Politics of American Urban Culture and Identity, 1910–1940" (Ph.D. dissertation, University of Chicago, 2000).

19. On moral reformers' relative disinterest in homosexuality before

the First World War, see Chauncey, *Gay New York*, 130, 137–141; on the temporary escalation of antigay policing during the war itself, see 141–149. On the rise of urban moral reform in general, see D'Emilio and Freedman, *Intimate Matters*, 150–156, 202–215; Chauncey, *Gay New York*, 137-141, 183–186, 197–198, 249–250; Boyer, *Urban Masses and Moral Order in America*, 191–219.

20. Havelock Ellis, *Sexual Inversion*, 3d ed. (Philadelphia: F. A. Davis, 1900), quoted in Chauncey, "From Sexual Inversion to Homosexuality: Medicine and the Changing Conceptualization of Female Deviance," *Salmagundi* (Fall 1982/Winter 1983): 114, 120–121; see ibid., 71, citing W. L. Howard, "Effeminate Men and Masculine Women," *New York Medical Journal* (1900).

21. W. C. Rivers, "A New Male Homosexual Trait (?)," *Alienist & Neurologist* (1920): 41, quote in Chauncey, "From Sexual Inversion to Homosexuality," 120. See also Charles Rosenberg and Carroll Smith-Rosenberg, "The Female Animal: Medical and Biological Views of Women," *Journal of American History* 60 (1973): 332.

22. See Chauncey, "From Sexual Inversion to Homosexuality;" Siobhan Somerville, "Scientific Racism and the Invention of the Homosexual Body," in *Queer Studies: A Lesbian, Gay & Transgender Anthology*, eds. Brett Beemyn and Mickey Eliason (New York: New York University Press, 1996), 241; D'Emilio and Freedman, *Intimate Matters*, 122, 226; Jennifer Terry, *An American Obsession: Science, Medicine, and Homosexuality in Modern Society* (Chicago: University of Chicago Press, 1999); Lisa Duggan, *Sapphic Slashers: Sex, Violence, and American Modernity* (Durham: Duke University Press, 2000).

23. Chauncey, *Gay New York*, chapter 12.

24. On the relationship between the depiction of communists and homosexuals, see Johnson, *Lavender Scare*. On the role of anti-Semitic discourse in shaping images of homosexuals as cosmopolitan outsiders, see my forthcoming book, *The Strange Career of the Closet*.

25. Chauncey, *Gay New York*, 359–360 (verbatim). See also Freedman, "'Uncontrolled Desires,'" especially 83, 92; Chauncey, "The Postwar Sex Crime Panic," 172; D'Emilio, *Sexual Politics, Sexual Communities*, chapter 3.

26. U.S. Congress, Senate, *Senate Report* 241, 81st Cong., 2d session,

1950, 3, 4, 5, 4. For a fuller analysis of Cold War era antigay rhetoric, see D'Emilio, "Homosexual Menace"; Johnson, *Lavender Scare*; and my forthcoming *The Strange Career of the Closet*.

Chapter 2

1. My account of postwar lesbian and gay life draws on my nearly completed book, *The Strange Career of the Closet: Gay Culture, Consciousness, and Politics from the Second World War to the Gay Liberation Era* (forthcoming from Basic Books); Elizabeth Lapovsky Kennedy and Madeline D. Davis, *Boots of Leather, Slippers of Gold: The History of a Lesbian Community* (New York: Routledge, 1993); Brett Beemyn, ed., *Creating a Place for Ourselves: Lesbian, Gay, and Bisexual Community Histories* (New York: Routledge, 1997); and John Loughery, *The Other Side of Silence: Men's Lives and Gay Identities: A Twentieth-Century History* (New York: Holt, 1998).

2. Allan Bérubé, *Coming Out Under Fire: The History of Gay Men and Women in World War Two* (New York: Free Press, 1990); David K. Johnson, *The Lavender Scare: The Cold War Persecution of Gays and Lesbians in the Federal Government* (Chicago: University of Chicago Press, 2004).

3. There is a growing literature on gay organizing in the 1950s. My account here draws especially on John D'Emilio, *Sexual Politics, Sexual Communities: The Making of a Homosexual Minority, 1940–1970* (Chicago: University of Chicago Press, 1981); Martin Meeker, "Behind the Mask of Respectability: Reconsidering the Mattachine Society and Male Homophile Practice, 1950s and 1960s," *Journal of the History of Sexuality* 10 (2001): 78–116; Eric Marcus, *Making History: The Struggle for Gay and Lesbian Equal Rights, 1945–1990: An Oral History* (New York: HarperCollins, 1992); and my discussion in *The Strange Career of the Closet*. On Frank Kameny and the Mattachine Society of Washington, see David K. Johnson, *The Lavender Scare: The Cold War Persecution of Gays and Lesbians in the Federal Government* (Chicago: University of Chicago Press, 2004).

4. The literature on Stonewall and the post-Stonewall era is too extensive to cite here. This section summarizes some of the arguments of

my forthcoming book, *Strange Career of the Closet*, on the origins of "coming out," the politics of gay liberation, and the relationship of both to other civil rights and ethnic movements. I draw also on John D'Emilio, "After Stonewall," in *Making Trouble: Essays on Gay History, Politics, and the University* (New York: Routledge, 1992), 224–274; D'Emilio, *The World Turned: Essays on Gay History, Politics, and Culture* (Durham: Duke University Press, 2002); and Toby Marotta, *The Politics of Homosexuality* (Boston: Houghton Mifflin, 1981).

5. I develop a fuller version of this argument in *The Strange Career of the Closet*.

6. This section draws again on *Strange Career of the Closet*; D'Emilio, "After Stonewall;" and Dudley Clendinen and Adam Nagourney, *Out for Good: The Struggle to Build a Gay Rights Movement in America* (New York: Simon and Schuster, 1999).

7. Ronald Bayer, *Homosexuality and American Psychiatry: The Politics of Diagnosis* (New York: Basic, 1981); Clendinen and Adam Nagourney, *Out for Good*, chapter 14; Gary B. Melton, "Public Policy and Private Prejudice," *American Psychologist* 44 (1989): 933. See "Resolution of the American Psychiatric Association, Dec. 15, 1973," in Ibid., appendix A, 936.

8. "Resolution of the Council of Representatives of the American Psychological Association," *American Psychologist* 30 (1975): 633.

9. A full list of the denominations issuing such statements is available in *Lawrence v. Texas*, No. 02–102 (June 26, 2003), Brief for Professors of History et al. as Amicus Curiae.

10. Johnson, *Lavender Scare*, chapter 8 and epilogue.

11. James W. Button, Barbara A. Rienzo, and Kenneth D. Wald, *Private Lives, Public Conflicts: Battles over Gay Rights in American Communities* (Washington, D.C.: Congressional Quarterly Press, 1997), chapter 3.

12. For a vivid account of the Dade County referendum campaign, see Clendinen and Nagourney, *Out for Good*, chapter 22.

13. Ibid., chapters 23–24.

14. The literature on AIDS is immense. My account in the following paragraphs draws on Randy Shilts, *And the Band Played On: Politics, People, and the AIDS Epidemic* (New York: St. Martin's Press, 1987);

Steven Epstein, *Impure Science: AIDS, Activism, and the Politics of Knowledge* (Berkeley: University of California Press, 1996); John-Manuel Andriote, *Victory Deferred: How AIDS Changed Gay Life in America* (Chicago: University of Chicago Press, 1999); and Cathy J. Cohen, *The Boundaries of Blackness: AIDS and the Breakdown of Black Politics* (Chicago: University of Chicago Press, 1999).

15. Nan Hunter, "Life After Hardwick," *Harvard Civil Rights—Civil Liberties Review* 27 (1992): 531–554.

16. NORC/General Social Survey tabulations, reported in Karlyn H. Bowman, *Attitudes About Homosexuality and Gay Marriage* (March 2002, updated February 13, 2004), available at American Enterprise Institute Online, http://www.aei.org/publications/pubID.14882,filter./pub_detail.asp.

17. On militant AIDS activism, see, for example, Douglas Crimp with Adam Rolston, *AIDS Demo Graphics* (Seattle, Wa.: Bay Press, 1990). My understanding of the political impact of people's shifting emotional responses to the epidemic is indebted to Deborah Gould, "Sex, Death, and the Politics of Anger: Emotions and Reason in ACT UP's Fight Against AIDS," Ph.D. dissertation, University of Chicago, 2000.

18. Button, Rienzo, and Wald, *Private Lives, Public Conflicts*, chapter 3.

19. Here I follow John Gallagher and Chris Bull, *Perfect Enemies: The Battle Between the Religious Right and the Gay Movement* (New York: Crown Publishers, 1996).

20. My account of the arguments made by antigay activists during the referendum campaigns draws on Didi Herman, *The Antigay Agenda: Orthodox Vision and the Christian Right* (Chicago: University of Chicago Press, 1997); Bull and Gallagher, *Perfect Enemies*; and Button, et al., *Private Lives, Public Conflicts*, chapter 6. On the referenda overturning civil rights laws, see Barbara S. Gamble, "Putting Civil Rights to a Popular Vote," *American Journal of Political Science* 41 (1997): 245–269. For an example of fair housing laws being attacked for giving "special protections" to African-Americans, see Thomas Sugrue, *The Origins of the Urban Crisis: Race and Inequality in Postwar Detroit* (Princeton: Princeton University Press, 1996), 227.

21. *Los Angeles Times* polling data, reported in Bowman, *Attitudes About Homosexuality and Gay Marriage*. See also *Los Angeles Times*,

"Americans Oppose Same-Sex Marriage but Acceptance of Gays in Society Grows," Poll Alert Study #501 press release, 11 April 2004.

22. Princeton Survey Research Associates/*Newsweek* survey tabulations, reported in Bowman, *Attitudes about Homosexuality and Gay Marriage*. See also *Los Angeles Times*, "Americans Oppose Same-Sex Marriage but Acceptance of Gays in Society Grows," Poll Alert Study #501 press release, 11 April 2004.

23. On Clinton, the 1992 election, and the military debate, see Gallagher and Bull, *Perfect Enemies*.

24. Again, see Gallagher and Bull, *Perfect Enemies*; Lisa Keen, "Referendums and Rights: Across the Country, Battles over Protections for Gays and Lesbians," *Washington Post*, 31 October 1993, C3; and Jane Schacter, "The Gay Civil Rights Debate in the States: Decoding the Discourse of Equivalents," *Harvard Civil Rights—Civil Liberties Law Review* 29 (1994): 289.

25. Donald P. Haider-Markel, "Lesbian and Gay Politics in the States: Interest Groups, Electoral Politics, and Policy," in Rimmerman et al., *The Politics of Gay Rights*, 290–346.

26. Kirstin Downey Grimsley, "Rights Group Rates Gay-Friendly Firms," *Washington Post*, 14 August 2002.

27. Wayne van der Meide, *Legislating Equality: A Review of Laws Affecting Gay, Lesbian, Bisexual, and Transgendered People in the United States* (Washington, D.C.: National Gay and Lesbian Task Force, 2000).

28. For a thoughtful critical review of the media, see Larry Gross, *Up from Invisibility: Lesbians, Gay Men, and the Media in America* (New York: Columbia University Press, 2001).

29. Gay and Lesbian Alliance Against Defamation, "Where We Are on TV," http://www.glaad.org/eye/ontv/index.php. On *thirtysomething*, see "Why China Beach Abortion Episode Won't Be Shown Again," *Chicago Sun-Times*, 30 July 1990, 47.

30. Polls showed that African-Americans were about 10 percent more disapproving of homosexuality behavior, and about 10 percent more supportive of equal employment rights. The best analysis of this complex of attitudes is provided by Alan Yang, *From Wrongs to Rights: Public Opinion on Gay and Lesbian Americans Moves Toward Equality* (New York: National Gay and Lesbian Task Force Policy Institute, 1 June

1998). See also the Gallup Poll results reported in Bowman, *Attitudes About Homosexuality and Gay Marriage*.

31. I draw here on Gregory B. Lewis and Jonathan L. Edelson, "DOMA and ENDA: Congress Votes on Gay Rights," in Rimmerman et al., *Politics of Gay Rights*, 193–216. On the pronounced regional variations in custody cases, see Donald H. Stone, "The Moral Dilemma: Child Custody When One Parent Is Homosexual or Lesbian—An Empirical Study," *Suffolk University Law Review* 23 (1989): 711–754.

Chapter 3

1. This chapter does not attempt to provide a comprehensive history of marriage, although that would be a worthy project, since almost every argument against same-sex marriage based on the institution's "timeless" or "natural" character is ignorant of marriage's actual history. The journalist E. J. Graff makes that clear in her lively, thorough and pointed guide to the often startling history of marriage, *What Is Marriage For?* (Boston: Beacon Press, 1999). She makes a number of the observations I do here, and many more, but throughout this chapter I have cited my first source, *Public Vows: A History of Marriage and the Nation* (Cambridge: Harvard University Press, 2000), by the eminent Harvard historian Nancy Cott. I highly recommend both books for those who wish to learn more. This chapter is also indebted to the Amici Curiae Brief of the Professors of the History of Marriage, Families, and the Law submitted in the Massachusetts marriage case, *Goodridge v. Department of Public Health*.

2. For a fuller account of such customary practices, see point no. 4.

3. Cott, *Public Vows*, 11–17.

4. Cott, *Public Vows*, 47–52.

5. Laura F. Edwards, "'The Marriage Covenant Is at the Foundation of All Our Rights': The Politics of Slave Marriages in North Carolina After Emancipation," *Law and History Review* 14 (1996): 81–124; Michael Grossberg, *Governing the Hearth: Law and the Family*

in Nineteenth-Century America (Chapel Hill: University of North Carolina Press, 1985), 129–136.

6. Peggy Pascoe, "Miscegenation Law, Court Cases, and Ideologies of 'Race' in Twentieth-Century America," *Journal of American History* 83 (1996): 44–69, quote at 49; Randall Kennedy, *Interracial Intimacies: Sex, Marriage, Identity, and Adoption* (New York: Pantheon, 2003), 79–85, 214–280, Congressional speech quoted at 85; Martha Hodes, *White Women, Black Men: Illicit Sex in the Nineteenth-Century South* (New Haven: Yale University Press, 1997).

7. Kennedy, *Interracial Intimacies*, 242–243; Mary Ann Glendon, *The Transformation of Family Law: State, Law, and Family in the United States and Western Europe* (Chicago: University of Chicago Press, 1989), 75–76, 80–82.

8. *Perez v. Sharp*, 32 Cal.2d 711, 717 (1948).

9. *Loving v. Virginia*, 388 U.S. 1, 12 (1967).

10. *Turner v. Safley*, 482 U.S. 78 (1987).

11. *Goodridge v. Department of Public Health*.

12. George Gallup, Jr., and Frank Newport, "For First Time, More Americans Approve of Interracial Marriage Than Disapprove," *Gallup Poll Monthly*, August 1991, 60. In 1965, 48 percent of white Americans and 72 percent of white Southerners approved of laws banning interracial marriage (*The Gallup Poll: Public Opinion, 1935–1971*, vol. 3 [New York: Random House, 1972], 1928). In 1993, 18 percent of whites still favored laws against interracial marriage (*Gallup Poll Monthly*, July 1993, 48).

13. Cott, *Public Vows*, 3.

14. John Demos, *A Little Commonwealth: Family Life in Plymouth Colony* (New York: Oxford University Press, 1970); Hendrik Hartog, *Man and Wife in America: A History* (Cambridge, Mass.: Harvard University Press, 2000), 99–101.

15. Cott, *Public Vows*, 67–68, 92–96; Amy Dru Stanley, *From Bondage to Contract: Wage Labor, Marriage, and the Market in the Age of Slave Emancipation* (New York: Cambridge University Press, 1998).

16. Aileen S. Kraditor, *The Ideas of the Woman Suffrage Movement, 1890–1920* (New York: Columbia University Press, 1965), 12–19.

17. Cott, *Public Vows*, 143–144, 165; Lizabeth Cohen, *A Consumers' Republic: The Politics of Mass Consumption in Postwar America* (New York:

Knopf, 2003); Alice Kessler-Harris, *In Pursuit of Equality: Women, Men, and the Quest for Economic Citizenship in 20th-Century America* (New York: Oxford University Press, 2001).

18. Cott, *Public Vows*, 206; Jennifer Wriggins, "Marriage Law and Family Law: Autonomy, Interdependence and Couples of the Same Gender," *Boston College Law Review* 41 (2000): 281–282.

19. Wriggins, "Marriage Law and Family Law," 304.

20. The historian Michael B. Katz provides very useful accounts of the development and current prospects of the American welfare state and social insurance systems in *In the Shadow of the Poorhouse: A Social History of Welfare in America* (New York: Basic Books, 1986) and *The Price of Citizenship: Redefining the American Welfare State* (New York: Metropolitan Books, 2001). See also *Women, the State, and Welfare*, edited by Linda Gordon (Madison: University of Wisconsin Press, 1990). A pioneering excellent account of the benefits denied same-sex couples was provided by David Chambers, "What If? The Legal Consequences of Marriage and the Legal Needs of Lesbian and Gay Male Couples," *Michigan Law Review* 95 (November 1996): 447–491.

21. General Accounting Office, Office of the General Counsel, Report to the Honorable Henry J. Hyde, Chairman, Committee on the Judiciary, House of Representatives, 31 January 1997 (GAO/OGC-97-16 Defense of Marriage Act).

22. Lizabeth Cohen, *A Consumers' Republic* (New York: Knopf, 2003), 137–146.

23. Cott, *Public Vows*, 190–193; Cohen, *Consumer's Republic*, 143–146.

24. On the development of the private welfare state, see Michael Katz, *The Price of Citizenship*, chapters 7, 10; Jennifer Klein, *For All These Rights: Business, Labor, and the Shaping of America's Public-Private Welfare State* (Princeton: Princeton University Press, 2003). For a survey of benefits received by workers and their significance in the compensation package, see Glenn M. Grossman, "U.S. Workers Receive a Wide Range of Employee Benefits," *Monthly Labor Review*, September 1992, 36–39, and Ann C. Foster, "Employee Benefits in the United States, 1991–92," *Compensation and Working Conditions* 46:7 (July 1994): 1–6.

25. GAO report; Wriggins, "Marriage Law and Family Law," 301; Lisa Bennett and Gary J. Gates, "The Cost of Marriage Inequality to Children and Their Same-Sex Parents" (Washington, D.C.: Human Rights Campaign Foundation Report, 13 April 2004).

26. "Older Gays Still Hesitant About Coming Out," *Boston Globe*, 11 January 2004; "Seniors, Home Care Advocates Voice Support for Gay Marriage," *Boston Globe*, 29 January 2004.

27. Michael Paulson, "Episcopal Diocese Sets Same-Sex Wedding Ban," *Boston Globe*, 13 May 2004.

28. A good overview of the process described in this and the following paragraph is provided by Glendon, *Transformation of Family Law*, 19–34, quotation at 24. See also James A. Brundage, *Law, Sex, and Christian Society in Medieval Europe* (Chicago: University of Chicago Press, 1987), 431–433, 553–558.

29. Grossberg, *Governing the Hearth*, 19, 65–68. See also the previous note.

30. Canon 1060, as quoted in Paul H. Besanceney, S. J., *Interfaith Marriages: Who and Why* (New Haven: College and University Press, 1970), 117.

31. C. Stanley Lowell, *Protestant-Catholic Marriage* (Nashville: Broadman Press, 1962), 1–2;. Besanceney, *Interfaith Marriages*, 118–119.

32. Lowell, *Protestant-Catholic Marriage*, 2; Besanceney, *Interfaith Marriages*, 118–119.

33. Lowell, *Protestant-Catholic Marriage*, 65.

34. On the New York debate over divorce reform, see Nelson Manfred Blake, *The Road to Reno: A History of Divorce in the United States* (New York: Macmillan, 1962), chapter 14; on the spread of no-fault divorce, see Glendon, *Transformation of Family Law: State, Law*, 188–196.

35. Gaines M. Foster, *Moral Reconstruction: Christian Lobbyists and the Federal Legislation of Morality, 1865–1920* (Chapel Hill: University of North Carolina Press, 2002), 49–54.

36. *Goodridge v. Department of Public Health*, quoting *Lawrence v. Texas*, 123 S. Ct. 2472, 2480 (2003) (Lawrence), which itself was quoting *Planned Parenthood of Southeastern Pa. v. Casey*, 505 U.S. 833, 850 (1992).

37. Glendon, *Transformation of Family Law*, 95, 283.

Chapter 4

1. Randy Lloyd, "Let's Push Homophile Marriage," *ONE*, June 1963, 5–9.

2. Quoted in Kay Tobin and Randy Wicker, *The Gay Crusaders* (New York: Paperback Library, 1972), 144; Don Teal, *The Gay Militants* (New York: Stein and Day, 1971), 282–293. *The Advocate* regularly reported on the burgeoning number of marriage cases. See, for instance, "Women to Fight for Kentucky License," *Advocate*, 5–18 August 1970; "'I Do' Rites Stir Hassle in New York," 12–25 May 1971; "Welfare Thinks They're Couple, But License Bureau Won't Agree," 29 September–12 October 1971; "Two Milwaukee Women Fight for Marriage License," 8 December 1971; "Black Lesbians' Wedding Crowded: Marriage License Lawsuit Stalled" and "Socialite Son Sues," 2 February 1972.

3. For a brilliant analysis of these early cases and the legislative response, see Peggy Pascoe, "Sex, Gender, and Same-Sex Marriage," in *Is Academic Feminism Dead?* edited by The Social Justice Group at The Center for Advanced Feminist Studies, University of Minnesota (New York: New York University Press, 2000), 86–129.

4. "'Marriage Is an Evil that Most Men Welcome,'" *Advocate*, March 29, 1972; MCC membership and marriage figures supplied in a personal communication from Jim Birkitt, MCC Communications Department, June 2004.

5. Quoted in Teal, *The Gay Militants*, 291.

6. On such friendship circles, see Kath Weston, *Families We Choose: Lesbians, Gays, Kinship* (New York: Columbia University Press, 1991) and Peter M. Nardi, *Gay Men's Friendships: Invincible Communities* (Chicago: University of Chicago Press, 1999).

7. Rhonda R. Rivera, "Lawyers, Clients, and AIDS: Some Notes from the Trenches," *Ohio State Law Journal* 49 (1989): 883–928.

8. Jeffrey G. Sherman, "Undue Influence and the Homosexual Testator," *University of Pittsburgh Law Review* 42 (1981): 225–267.

9. My account of this case follows that provided by David L. Chambers, "Tales of Two Cities: AIDS and the Legal Recognition of Domestic Partnerships in San Francisco and New York," *Law & Sexuality* 2 (1992): 194–199.

10. Again, I follow the superb analysis provided by Chambers, "Tales of Two Cities," 181–208.

11. A brief explanation of those technologies may be in order for readers unfamiliar with them. By the 1970s, the technology for freezing and thawing sperm had been in use for more than twenty years. Lesbians in the 1980s were able to purchase frozen sperm from sperm banks in major cities and, with their doctor's help, be inseminated with it and become pregnant. The technology for combating infertility, initially intended for married heterosexual couples, continued to develop in the 1970s and 1980s, and continues to develop today. In 1978, a child was born for the first time through in vitro fertilization. In IVF, doctors remove eggs from a woman's ovaries and combine the eggs with sperm in hopes of fertilizing the eggs. If fertilization occurs, after several days some 'preembryos' are placed back in a woman's uterus where it is hoped they will grow to maturity. This procedure, while expensive, became more widely available in the 1980s and 1990s. In 1982, the Sperm Bank of California was created to cater primarily to unmarried heterosexual women and lesbians. See Lori B. Andrews, *The Clone Age: Adventures in the New World of Reproductive Technology* (New York: Henry Holt, 1999).

12. My account of the lesbian baby boom, the legal issues it raised, and the issues confronting lesbian and gay parents in custody disputes that arose upon their divorce from other-sex partners relies on Nancy D. Polikoff, "This Child Does Have Two Mothers: Redefining Parenthood to Meet the Needs of Children in Lesbian-Mother and Other Nontraditional Families," *Georgetown Law Journal* 78 (1990): 459–575; Julie Shapiro, "Custody and Conduct: How the Law Fails Lesbian and Gay Parents and Their Children," *Indiana Law Journal* 71 (1996) 623–627; and Jane S. Schacter, "Constructing Families in a Democracy: Courts, Legislatures and Second-Parent Adoption," *Chicago-Kent Law Review* 75 (2000): 933–950.

13. Amy D. Ronner, "*Bottoms v. Bottoms:* The Lesbian Mother and the Judicial Perpetuation of Damaging Stereotypes," *Yale Journal of Law and Feminism* 7 (1995): 341–373. For examples of the wide publicity given the case, see "Gay Parents: Under Fire and on the Rise,"

Time, 20 September 1993, 66; "Fighting for Tyler: A Lesbian Loses Her Son to Her Own Mother," *People*, 27 September 1993, 71.

14. Donald H. Stone, "The Moral Dilemma: Child Custody When One Parent Is Homosexual or Lesbian—An Empirical Study," *Suffolk University Law Review* 23 (1989): 727.

15. Quoted in Stone, "The Moral Dilemma," 741–742.

16. Ellen C. Perrin, M.D., and the Committee on Psychosocial Aspects of Child and Family Health, American Academy of Pediatrics, "Technical Report: Coparent or Second-Parent Adoption by Same-Sex Parents," *Pediatrics* 109 (2002): 341–344.

17. Casey Charles, *The Sharon Kowalski Case: Lesbian and Gay Rights on Trial* (Lawrence: University Press of Kansas, 2003).

18. John Simons, "Gay Marriage, Corporate America Blazed the Trail," *Fortune*, 2 June 2004. But see also "What's News," *Wall Street Journal*, 14 August 2002, and "Business Brief," *Wall Street Journal*, 23 June 2000. Human Rights Campaign, WorkNet Database, http://www. hrc.org/worknet/dp/index.asp (accessed 17 May 2004). Mychal Judge Police & Fire Chaplains Public Safety Officers' Benefit Act of 2002, Public Law No. 107–196, 116 Stat. 719 (24 June 2002).

19. The printed record of the feminist debate is immense, but I describe the exchange between Polikoff and Hunter because they articulated widely shared positions with great thoughtfulness. See Nan D. Hunter, "Marriage, Law, and Gender: A Feminist Inquiry," *Law & Sexuality* 1 (1991), 1–30, and Nancy D. Polikoff, "We Will Get What We Ask For: Why Legalizing Gay and Lesbian Marriage Will Not Dismantle the Legal Structure of Gender in Every Marriage," *Virginia Law Review* 79 (1993), 1535–1550.

20. As with the feminist debate, this debate was, of course, more wide-ranging and nuanced than a short sketch can suggest. Key texts include Andrew Sullivan, "Here Comes the Groom: A Conservative Case for Gay Marriage," *New Republic*, 28 August 1989, 20–22, an argument later amplified in his book *Virtually Normal: An Argument About Homosexuality* (New York: Knopf, 1995); Jonathan Rauch, "For Better or Worse?," *New Republic*, 6 May 1996, 18–23, since amplified in his book, *Gay Marriage: Why It Is Good for Gays, Good for Straights, and Good for America* (New York: Holt, 2004); Michael Warner, *The Trouble with*

Normal: Sex, Politics, and the Ethics of Queer Life (New York: Free Press, 1999). *Same-Sex Marriage: Pro and Con: A Reader*, edited by Andrew Sullivan (New York: Vintage, 1997), is a good place to start for people interested in following the intricacies of the early debates over marriage. It includes excerpts from Sullivan and Rauch's writing.

21. For a good review of the literature on assimilation, see Russell A. Kazal, "Revisiting Assimilation: The Rise, Fall, and Reappraisal of a Concept in American History," *American Historical Review* 100 (1995): 437–471. For recent work arguing for a more complex analysis of the process, see, e.g., Ulf Hannerz, "The World in Creolization," *Africa* 57 (1987): 546–559; Kathleen Conzen, "Mainstreams and Side Channels: The Localization of Immigrant Cultures," *Journal of American Ethnic History* 11 (Fall 1991): 5–20; Kathleen Conzen et al., "The Invention of Ethnicity: A Perspective from the U.S.A.," *Journal of Ethnic History* 12 (Fall 1992): 3–41; Frances R. Aparicio and Susana Chávez-Silverman, editors, *Tropicalizations: Transcultural Representations of Latinidad* (Hanover, NH: University Press of New England, 1997).

22. David Chambers, "What If? The Legal Consequences of Marriage and the Legal Needs of Lesbian and Gay Male Couples," *Michigan Law Review* 95 (November 1996): 447–491.

23. Brief of Plaintiffs-Appellants, *Goodridge v. Department of Public Health*.

24. Amici Curiae Brief of Charles Kindregan, Jr., and Monroe Inker. Available at http://www.glad.org/marriage/goodridge_amici. shtml.

25. Amici Curiae Brief of the Massachusetts Psychiatric Society, the Massachusetts Psychological Association, the American Psychoanalytic Association, the National Association of Social Workers, the Massachusetts Chapter of the National Association of Social Workers, the Boston Psychoanalytical Society and Institute, Inc., the Massachusetts Association for Psychoanalytic Psychology, the Gottman Institute, Barry Zuckerman, M.D., Evian D. Frantz III, M.D., Ellen C. Perrin, M.D., and Judith Palfrey, M.D. Available at http://www.glad.org/ marriage/goodridge_amici.shtml.

26. Perrin, "Technical Report: Coparent or Second-Parent Adoption by Same-Sex Parents."

27. American Psychological Association, *Lesbian and Gay Parenting: A Resource for Psychologists* (Washington, D.C.: APA, 1995).

28. Quoting Charlotte J. Patterson, "Family Relationships of Lesbians and Gay Men," *Journal of Marriage and the Family* 62 (2000): 1053.

29. Amici Curiae Brief of the Massachusetts Psychiatric Society et al.

30. Descriptions of the plaintiffs come from the Plaintiffs' Complaint in *Goodridge v. Department of Public Health*, filed in Suffolk Superior Court, 11 April 2001.

31. *Goodridge v. Department of Public Health*.

Chapter 5

1. "San Francisco Sees Tide Shift in the Battle over Marriage," *New York Times*, 12 March 2004, A12.

2. Karen Vreslau and Brad Stone, "Outlaw Vows," *Newsweek*, 1 March 2004, 43.

3. For statistical analysis of the couples getting licenses in Massachusetts, see Scott S. Greenberger and Bill Dedman, "Survey Finds Women In Majority," *Boston Globe*, 18 May 2004; for San Francisco, see Suzanne Herel, Rona Marech, and Ilene Lelchuk, "Numbers Put Face on a Phenomenon: Most Who Married Are Middle-Aged, Have College Degrees," *San Francisco Chronicle*, 18 March 2004. No statistics were collected on the racial backgrounds of the couples, although several observers commented they were overwhelmingly white.

4. For an excellent introduction to the politics of the groups leading the campaign against marriage equality in Massachusetts (and nationally), see Sean Cahill, "Anti-Gay Groups Active in Massachusetts: A Closer Look" (New York: National Gay and Lesbian Task Force Policy Institute, 2004), available at http://www.thetaskforce.org/downloads/AntiGayMA.pdf. The 1996 Southern Baptist Convention resolution is available at http://www.religioustolerance.org/new1_966.htm

5. This issue has been explored in several studies of the ERA. My argument here follows Pascoe's analysis in "Sex, Gender, and Same-Sex Marriage," in *Is Academic Feminism Dead?* ed. The Social Justice

Group at The Center for Advanced Feminist Studies, University of Minnesota (New York: New York University Press, 2000), 86–129.

6. Nancy T. Ammerman, "North American Protestant Fundamentalism," in *Fundamentalisms Observed*, vol. 1, edited by Martin E. Marty and R. Scott Appleby (Chicago: University of Chicago Press, 1991), 1–65.

7. Jerry Falwell, *Listen, America!* (Garden City, N.Y.: Doubleday, 1980), 183.

8. Ibid., 185.

9. Glenn T. Stanton, "Is Marriage in Jeopardy?" available at http://www.family.org, 27 August 2003; updated 10 September 2003.

10. See Karlyn H. Bowman, *Attitudes About Homosexuality and Gay Marriage* (March 2002, updated 13 February 2004), available at American Enterprise Institute Online, http://www.aei.org/publications/pubID.14882,filter./pub_detail.asp; and Jeffrey Schmalz, "Poll Finds an Even Split on Homosexuality's Cause," *New York Times*, 5 March 1993, A14.

11. See Bowman, *Attitudes About Homosexuality and Gay Marriage*, and Schmalz, "Poll Finds an Even Split on Homosexuality's Cause."

12. Michel Foucault, *The History of Sexuality*, trans. Robert Hurley (New York: Pantheon Books, 1978), 43. I increasingly think that a major error of most post-Foucaultian histories of sexuality has been to assume the triumph of this modernist view of sexual identity.

13. Two major polling studies in late 2003 and early 2004 reported the correlation between attitudes toward homosexuals, religious belief, and belief about the mutability of sexual orientation, and I draw on their statistics in the following discussion: The Pew Research Center for the People and the Press and the Pew Forum on Religion and Public Life, "Religious Beliefs Underpin Opposition to Homosexuality: Republicans United, Democrats Split on Gay Marriage," news release, 18 November 2003; and *Los Angeles Times*, "Americans Oppose Same-Sex Marriage but Acceptance of Gays in Society Grows," Poll Alert Study #501 press release, 11 April 2004. See also Didi Herman, *The Antigay Agenda: Orthodox Vision and the Christian Right* (Chicago: University of Chicago Press, 1997).

14. Neil A. Lewis, "From the Rose Garden: Same-Sex Marriage;

Bush Backs Bid to Block Gays from Marrying," *New York Times*, 31 July 2003, A1.

15. Congress, Senate, Senator John Ashcroft of Missouri, 104th Cong., 2d sess., *Congressional Record* (6 September 1996), vol. 142, S10000.

16. My discussion of the Christian Right's political uses of "reparative therapy" is based on Surina Khan, "Calculated Compassion: How The Ex-Gay Movement Serves The Right's Attack on Democracy" (Political Research Associates, Policy Institute of the National Gay and Lesbian Task Force, and Equal Partners in Faith, 1998), available at http://www.publiceye.org/equality/x-gay/X-Gay.html#P2_0.

17. Other commentaries on the relationship between the bans on interracial marriage and same-sex marriage include Andrew Koppelman, "The Miscegenation Analogy: Sodomy Law as Sex Discrimination," *Yale Law Journal* 98 (1988): 145–164; and James Trosino, "American Wedding: Same-Sex Marriage and the Miscegenation Analogy," *Boston University Law Review* 73 (1993): 93–120.

18. Ariel [Buckner H. Payne], *The Negro: What Is His Ethnological Status?* (1867), in John David Smith, *The "Ariel" Controversy: Religion and "The Negro Problem"* (New York, 1993), as quoted in Jane Dailey, "Sex, Segregation, and the Sacred after *Brown*," *Journal of American History* 91 (2004): 119–144.

19. Historical accounts of "segregationist theology" include Jane Dailey, "Sex, Segregation, and the Sacred;" Andrew Michael Manis, *Southern Civil Religions in Conflict: Black and White Baptists and Civil Rights, 1954–1957* (Athens, Ga.: University of Georgia Press, 1987); and Bill J. Leonard, "A Theology for Racism: Southern Fundamentalists and the Civil Rights Movement," in *Southern Landscapes*, edited by Tony Badger, Walter Edgar, and Jan Nordby Gretlunds (Tübingen: Stauffenburg, 1996), 165–181.

20. The Virginia and Florida court decisions are quoted by Dailey, who also explains their reliance on Paul. See "Sex, Segregation, and the Sacred."

21. Jerry Falwell's sermon and later commentary on it were quoted by Nina Totenberg in "Jerry Falwell Reflects on Race, Sexuality in the U.S.A.," a segment on NPR's Morning Edition, broadcast 28 May 1996.

22. Congress, Senate, Senator Jesse Helms of North Carolina, 104th Cong., 2d sess., Congressional Record (9 September 1996), vol. 142, S10067; Charles Carroll, *The Tempter of Eve, or, The Criminality of Man's Social, Political, and Religious Equality with the Negro, and the Amalgamation to Which These Crimes Inevitably Lead* (St. Louis: The Adamic Publishing Co., 1902), as discussed in Dailey, "Sex, Segregation, and the Sacred."

23. Congress, Senate, Senator Byrd of West Virginia, 104th Cong., 2d sess., *Congressional Record* (10 September 1996), vol. 142, S10109; Early Van Deventer, *Perfection of the Races*, 1954 pamphlet quoted by Dailey, "Sex, Segregation, and the Sacred."

24. Dailey, "Sex, Segregation, and the Sacred."

25. James Weldon Johnson, *Along This Way* (New York: Viking, 1933), 170.

26. "Court Will Consider Miscegenation Laws," *Christian Century*, 27 May 1964, 693.

27. Gunnar Myrdal, *An American Dilemma: The Negro Problem and Modern Democracy* (New York: Harper & Brothers, 1944), 591.

28. Representative Canady of Florida, Representative Smith of Texas, 104th Cong., 2d sess., *Congressional Record* (12 July 1996), vol. 142, pp. H7491 and H7494, respectively.

Index

Index